Pie in the Sky

Pie in the Sky

How Joe Hill's Lawyers Lost His Case, Got Him Shot, and Were Disbarred

KENNETH LOUGEE

iUniverse, Inc.
Bloomington

Pie in the Sky
How Joe Hill's Lawyers Lost His Case, Got Him Shot, and Were Disbarred

iUniverse books may be ordered through booksellers or by contacting:

iUniverse
1663 Liberty Drive
Bloomington, IN 47403
www.iuniverse.com
1-800-Authors (1-800-288-4677)

Because of the dynamic nature of the Internet, any web addresses or links contained in this book may have changed since publication and may no longer be valid. The views expressed in this work are solely those of the author and do not necessarily reflect the views of the publisher, and the publisher hereby disclaims any responsibility for them.

Any people depicted in stock imagery provided by Thinkstock are models, and such images are being used for illustrative purposes only.
Certain stock imagery © Thinkstock.

ISBN: 978-1-4620-2992-1 (sc)
ISBN: 978-1-4620-2993-8 (hc)
ISBN: 978-1-4620-2994-5 (ebk)

Library of Congress Control Number: 2011910075

Printed in the United States of America

iUniverse rev. date: 08/30/2011

To Jan, who put up with this obsession.

To Ned Siegfried, Mitch Jensen, and Joe Steele, who believed in me and gave me a chance.

CONTENTS

Preface

It seems to me that at this time we need education in the obvious more than investigation of the obscure.

Justice Oliver Wendell Holmes

Joe Hill, the labor songwriter, was executed by the state of Utah on November 19, 1915, for a murder he may or may not have committed. For the past ninety years, pundits have argued guilt or innocence, a project not sustainable by either law or history.

Joe Hill was a remarkable individual. He was accused of a crime that his supporters, then and now, attribute to labor difficulties. It is certain that the trial took place under unfavorable labor circumstances. It is also clear that the Utah authorities saw the Joseph Hillstrom case (as they knew it) as an ordinary murder. It is the tension between these views that makes this case of interest in the twenty-first century.

More than any other labor defendant, Joe Hill remains vital to the national debate on the rights of working people. During the recent Wisconsin public union demonstrations, the employees sang the famous Joe Hill song "There Is Power in a Union." It is relevant to ask what Joe Hill would have thought about the use of his song by a well-fed, well-educated group of white-collar government workers. It would certainly be confusing, but once he understood the context, I have to believe he would have approved. Joe Hill would have responded to the public employees' strike with wit and keen understanding. He would have then written a brilliant song for the occasion.

II

I Dreamed I Saw Joe Hill

Given the current relevance of Joe Hill to the labor movement, it is hard to believe how long it has been since his trial and execution. The murder of the Morrison father and son occurred in January 1914.

At the time, Theodore Roosevelt was descending the River of Doubt in Brazil. Woodrow Wilson was in his first administration. Franklin Roosevelt was undersecretary of the navy. There were no antibiotics. Polio, malaria, and numerous other ailments still plagued humankind.

The murder of the Austrian Archduke Franz Ferdinand occurred as the Joe Hill trial was concluding. A month later, World War I erupted. While Utah was focused on the Joe Hill appeal in the Utah Supreme Court and the efforts for commutation, the Australians and New Zealanders suffered and died on the Gallipoli peninsula. By the time Hill's lawyer, Judge Orin Hilton, was disbarred, the French and German armies had bled themselves at Verdun and the British had lost over a million men at the Battle of the Somme. Literally millions of men were wounded or dying in the first holocaust of the twentieth century. This bloodletting went almost unnoticed in Utah, where the Joe Hill matter took top billing.

Since the Joe Hill trial, the American people have experienced World War I, the Roaring Twenties, the Great Depression, World War II, Korea, Senator McCarthy, Vietnam, Watergate, the revolt in Iran, and two wars in the Persian Gulf. The labor movement has produced the CIO, John L. Lewis, and George Meany. Fifteen men have served as president. We have seen the beginning and the end of the Soviet Union.

Yet, Joe Hill has continuing interest and ability to inspire. The following song was sung by Miss Joan Baez at an Iraq war protest in Washington, DC in 2005. Miss Baez adapted the words of a song "I dreamed I saw Joe Hill Last Night." She compared Joe Hill to the mothers who had lost their sons in the war. The Joe Hill song was used to demonstrate the spirit of social protest. [1]

I dreamed I saw Joe Hill last night
Alive as you and me.
Says I, "But Joe you're ten years dead,"
"I never died" says he,
"I never died" says he.

"In Salt Lake City, Joe" says I to him,
Him standing by my bed,
"They framed you on a murder charge,"
Says Joe, "But I ain't dead."
Says Joe, "But I ain't dead."

"The copper bosses killed you, Joe.
They shot you, Joe," says I.
"Takes more than guns to kill a man,"
Says Joe, "I didn't die."
Says Joe, "I didn't die."

And standing there as big as life
And smiling with his eyes,
Joe says, "What they forgot to kill
Went on to organize,
Went on to organize."

"Joe Hill ain't dead," he says to me,
"Joe Hill ain't never dead.
Where workingmen defend their rights,
Joe Hill is on their side,
Joe Hill is on their side."

"From Crawford, Texas up to Washington,
In every mine and mill,
Where working men defend their rights
It's there you'll find Joe Hill,
It's there you find Joe Hill."

I dreamed I saw Joe Hill last night,
Alive as you or me,

Says I, "But Joe, you're ten years dead,"
"I never died," says he.
"I never died," says he.

III

The Stories We Tell

Given the continued vitality of Joe Hill, it is surprising how little is known of the actual crime and trial. Much of this can be explained by the histories that have been written on the case. The historiography of Joe Hill is limited but interesting. The song Joan Baez sang was written in 1930 by Alfred Hayes, a British-American screenwriter and poet. Hayes blames Joe Hill's execution on the "copper bosses."

In 1951, an internationally renowned playwright, Barrie Stavis, wrote a play, *The Man Who Never Died*, in which he claimed Joe Hill wouldn't tell where he was shot because he was having an affair with the wife of a copper boss. This play has been produced both in New York and throughout the world. It was particularly popular in the former Soviet Union.

In 1950, Wallace Stegner, the Utah writer, wrote a historical novel originally called *The Preacher and the Slave*, in which he concluded that Joe Hill was guilty. This caused the remnants of the IWW and other radical labor movements to picket his publisher. Like Stavis, Stegner relied upon fictional inventions to support his point of view.

The only professional historian to write on the Joe Hill matter was Dr. Philip Foner in 1965. Dr. Foner's book was entitled *The Case of Joe Hill*. Dr. Foner held a PhD from Columbia. He taught at New York University before he was fired in the McCarthy era for being a communist. He spent the remainder of his life writing for International Press, which was run by the Communist Party. Dr. Foner was a respectable professional historian, and the format of all of his footnotes is right.[2] His opinion was that because Joe Hill was a worker, he could not possibly be guilty. Dr. Foner concludes that the state of Utah should put up a monument in Sugarhouse Park that says, "Here Joe Hill was judicially murdered by the State of Utah."[3]

The last book is *Joe Hill*. It was written by Gibbs Smith and published by the University of Utah Press in 1967. Much primary material may be found in Smith's book. If you want to know about Joe Hill's life in Sweden or you want to look at the primary documents, Gibbs Smith's is a good place to start. Unfortunately, Mr. Smith was not a lawyer, and like all of the writers, made fundamental legal errors.

III

Law and the Trial Lawyer

Substantive constitutional law has changed in the last century. Most people today are familiar with the 1966 case, *Miranda v. Arizona,* in which the Supreme Court set out the easily recognized right to remain silent. Of equal importance was *Gideon v. Wainwright,* the 1963 case granting the accused the right to trial counsel. Further the Court decided *Mapp v. Ohio,* protecting the accused from unlawful search and seizure.

Joe Hill would have been entitled to the benefit of all of these important constitutional rights. For example, Hill was unrepresented at arraignment and at the preliminary hearing. Today, the government would provide him with a public defender. The police questioned him at length without giving him the *Miranda* warnings. His lodging place was searched without a proper warrant. In those respects, one can say with assurance that Joe Hill's rights would have been protected today.

There are elements of the American trial system that have not changed since 1914. The primary example is the law of evidence that has proved remarkably stable. Dean John Henry Wigmore prepared his *Treatise on the Anglo American System of Evidence in Trials at Common Law* in 1904. Wigmore's evidence rules are the basis for the *Federal Rules of Evidence* adopted in 1975. Virtually every state has adopted those rules, which are not significantly different from the pronouncements of Dean Wigmore.

Because the rules were stable, today's lawyers are able to evaluate how the Joe Hill trial was handled by the courts. Nonadmissible evidence would still not be allowed before the jury.

These stable evidentiary rules explain the actions of Judge Morris Ritchie in the Joe Hill matter. For example, Dr. Foner complains that the defense was not allowed to introduce the testimony of a newspaperman. That newspaperman was to testify as to conversations he had with the decedent, Mr. Morrison. Mr. Morrison supposedly told the reporter of the identity of several men who had threatened him or were angry with him because of actions taken while Morrison was on the Salt Lake City police force. The reason Judge Ritchie did not allow this evidence has nothing to do with prejudice by the court against Joe Hill. It is hearsay, not subject to any exception, and would be excluded today under the federal rules.

The same evidentiary rules explain the exclusion of evidence from individuals who thought Hill guilty. Professor Vernon Jensen, a labor historian at Cornell University, recorded that the doctor who treated Hill said that Joe Hill told him that he was guilty of the Morrison murders. In this case, the proposed evidence is not only hearsay but double hearsay. The reason why the courts do not allow the introduction of hearsay is because the *witness* has no firsthand experience supporting his testimony. Requiring firsthand knowledge is a rule of fairness and has always been present.

Another stable evidentiary issue found in Joe Hill's case is the concept of relevance. Hill and his lawyers wanted to argue that the fact he was shot the evening of the robbery was irrelevant to the issue of guilt. Again, the rules promulgated by Dean Wigmore made relevance a very low hurdle for Elmer Leatherwood, the prosecutor. All he had to show was that the wound had some tendency to show that Joe Hill was in fact the robber. Allowing evidence of the wound to be presented to the jury was not a sign of judicial prejudice by Judge Ritchie. It was recognition of established rules of evidence as set out by Dean Wigmore. The same result would be found in today's courts.

Another example of judicial stability is the concept of discretion by the trial judge to make decisions as to the admissibility of evidence. The Joe Hill appellate decision was largely concerned with the exercise of judicial discretion. For example, Hill's lawyers wanted to introduce evidence from a firearms expert. The proposed testimony was that Joe Hill's wound came from a steel bullet and not the lead bullet found in the decedent's weapon.

The expert had not seen Hill's wound for several months and had never made that determination before Hill's trial. The Utah Supreme Court upheld Judge Ritchie's decision to exclude that evidence because it was within Judge Ritchie's discretion to determine if such evidence was reliable and would assist the jury. Again, that decision would be committed to a trial judge under the modern rules of evidence.

Just as the law of evidence has remained stable, the art of the trial lawyer has not changed over the century. I have been watching trials and trial lawyers for over thirty years. In law school, I often ignored my class assignments to sneak down to the Lane County Courthouse to watch trials. I watched both civil and criminal trials. In my early professional life, I watched a number of trials from beginning to end. I learned to distinguish able trial lawyers from their less-accomplished brothers and sisters.

The latest thinking on trial practice is found in a book entitled *Reptile: The 2009 Manual of the Plaintiff's Revolution.*[4] The authors emphasize that the trial lawyer has to tell a compelling story of why the opposing party violated "rules" that are significant to the community. In other words, the trial lawyer demonstrates how people (in Joe Hill's case, the police) are supposed to act. Then she demonstrates that the police did not act in the appropriate manner. The Joe Hill trial lawyers failed to tell the jury a compelling story of innocence. In this respect, modern trial law theory explains the result.

What is lacking from the Joe Hill controversy is a balanced discussion of the actions of the lawyers and judges involved. They acted in predictable ways familiar to today's trial lawyers. A trial lawyer can recognize that the failure of the Joe Hill case depended as much upon the actions of his lawyers as it did on community prejudice. It is as if the people who have written on this case do not understand the scorecard. It is very difficult to determine what happened in that case without understanding the basis for the actions taken. When stable evidentiary rules and legal procedure are considered, today's trial lawyer finds serious fault in the handling of the matter.

IV

A Trial in Mormon Country

As a trial lawyer, I do not apologize for explanation of evidence and legal procedure. Likewise, I do not apologize for the treatment of Mormon history. My colleague at the bar, Mike Martinez, tells me that the "Mormons" executed Joe Hill. Mormonism is only part of the Joe Hill story, but it is a large part of the story.

In a discussion of Mormonism in the Joe Hill case, the problem is turning from the founding myths of the religion to a discussion of how Mormons behaved in society.[5] In this book, the particular problem is how Mormons behaved in the progressive era. I find continuity in Church doctrine that explains underlying assumptions and prejudices of the Latter-day Saints involved in the trial. I also find that the Utah non-Mormons, who were by far more important in Utah legal circles, took actions best explained by their residence in a primarily Mormon state.

I cannot tell a Utah story about trial law without confronting the Church. It is just and fair to talk about the Church and its members in connection with the Joe Hill story. The Church is important to the story because the trial, the appeal, the Utah hearings of the Utah Commutation Board, as well as the disbarment proceedings against Judge Hilton cannot be understood without evaluating the assumptions of the people living in Mormon Utah. There is no evidence that the Church leadership had anything to say for or against Joe Hill. But the Mormons had created a Utah society where assumptions, beliefs, and perceptions were commonly held by the members at large.

A trial lawyer must deal with assumptions and perceptions that in his world are real. At the turn of the twentieth century, physical scientists thought they were dealing only with empirical observations that could be replicated. The historians thought they were collecting facts which could not be disputed. As it turned out, the trial lawyers were not dealing with Newton's principles. Instead, they were dealing with relativity and chaos theory.

The Joe Hill matter does not proceed logically from fixed points of reference. Labor, management, Mormons, non-Mormons, lawyers, and jurors all came to this case with particular assumptions. The tragic result of the Joe Hill proceedings was not derived from the "facts" or logic. At its core, trial law reflects life, and life rarely follows a linear path.

V

The Truth Matters

In assuming Joe Hill innocent, labor and its supporters assume unfairness in the trial. Assuming Joe Hill guilty unjustly condemns the labor movement. Neither assumption is sustainable. All that can be done is to respectively view the actors, giving due deference to the historical and legal background.

The discussion of Joe Hill's trial without consideration of legal advocacy and Mormon history is akin to a discussion of Civil War battles without appreciation of the killing range of the rifled musket. It is impossible to discern fairness among the accused, their prosecutors, defenders, or judges without a proper consideration of the ideology or conditions under which the trial lawyers labored.

The theory of American trial law is that truth emerges from the clash of evidence and ideas. In Joe Hill's case, the issues and elements of trial law and Mormon history continued to clash through the century. While it would be presumptuous to arrive at resolution, we can examine at length the issues, trusting that fairness may emerge.

When he concurred with the disbarment of Joe Hill's lawyer, Judge Hilton, Justice Frick warned history as well as Hilton that fairness is fleeting. "If respondent's sympathies are so strong for human frailties, he should not lavish all of them upon those alone accused of crime. He should have some little regard for those whose duty it is to deal with that class. All are entitled to fair treatment ..."[6]

Acknowledgments

This short work originated as a presentation given to the Labor and Employment Section of the Utah State Bar Association in commemoration of the ninety-fifth anniversary of the execution of the labor leader, Joe Hill. It originated two years before. I was performing legal research on an issue of legal ethics. Using the legal research database *Westlaw*, I came across the case in which Joe Hill's last lawyer, Judge Orin Hilton, was disbarred by the Utah Supreme Court in 1916. Fascinated, I then read the Joe Hill decision. It became clear to me that there was more to this story than the conventional view that his conviction was a judicial lynching.

It was perhaps inevitable that I should come across the Joe Hill story. Fifteen years of practicing trial and appellate law in Alaska had sharpened my sense of what was normal procedure in the trial courts. I then attended graduate school in history at the University of Utah. Despite the best efforts of the faculty, my brain remained firmly cemented in the progressive era. Professor Dean May introduced me to the New Mormon History Movement. I developed an interest in historical Utah legal practice and procedure. My thesis was on early bankruptcy filings in northern Utah.

As I read the traditional works on the Joe Hill case, supplemented by readings in the secondary literature of labor in the intermountain west, the guilt or innocence of Joe Hill became more and more irrelevant. I became interested in the story of the sincere but incompetent Ernest MacDougall who represented Joe Hill in the trial court. Equally interesting was the venal and incompetent Frank B. Scott, who assisted MacDougall.

There was also the relentless prosecutor, Elmer Leatherwood, who took advantage of all of the defense lawyers' blunders. There was the Mormon jury foreman, Joseph Kimball, who was willing to answer all preliminary questions about the presumption of innocence without either the defense lawyers or history learning his parentage. There was the arrogant brilliance of Judge Orin Hilton, who represented Joe Hill after conviction. Hilton thought he could sway the Utah Supreme Court as he had swayed juries throughout the west without accounting for the rules of appellate procedure. There was the formal legalism of Chief Justice Daniel Straup, who never considered Oliver Wendell Holmes's observation that all judicial decisions rest upon public policy. I saw the political weakness of Governor William Spry, who did not and could not appreciate the damage done to the state by the execution. Most of all, I found Joe Hill dominating the story. He was fully grown in class and labor consciousness but incredibly naive as to the legal process and constitutional rights. In the end, it appeared to me that if he was innocent, he cared more about his legacy than his life.

There are other themes that arose in this study. The progressive era was a difficult period in Utah history. By the closest of margins, the Latter-day Saints avoided the fate of a footnote in history when Reed Smoot retained his senate seat. During the period of the Joe Hill trial, Mormons and non-Mormons warily edged toward accommodation. The tragic end of Joe Hill can only be fully explained by the predominance of non-Mormon lawyers in the judiciary. At all times, the non-Mormon lawyers, such as Justice Straup, were reminded of the Mormon electorate upon whom they depended for their offices. They were equally interested in demonstrating their independence from the influence of the Church. Both Mormon and non-Mormon views must be considered in reaching the results of the case.

I apologize for the familiar voice used in this book. It is perhaps natural, as this writing originated as a speech. I have edited the speech, supplemented where necessary, and added the references. I believe that my research will be valuable to historians of the west and the labor movement. I have tried to write in nonlegal terms to appeal to the lay reader interested in the Joe Hill matter. However, there are legal arguments that may appeal to the practitioner. So that the case law may be more available, I have retained the normal legal citation form.

There are numerous legal sources now available to the investigator. There were three documents authored by Chief Justice Daniel Straup, including *State v. Hillstrom*. That was the case name that Joe Hill was tried under by the Utah authorities.[7] No one in Utah knew the defendant by any other name. The commutation board also issued a lengthy opinion authored by Justice Straup. It is in the *Utah Digital Archives* and is available online. Finally, the court disbarred Joe Hill's last lawyer, Judge Orin Hilton. That case is entitled *In re Hilton*.[8]

We also have the letters that Joe Hill wrote to the newspapers and the commutation board. Most of the Utah newspapers are now available online in a project called *Utah Digital Newspapers*. This project does not include all of the *Tribune* or the *Deseret News* for good portions of the twentieth century, but they have every local paper throughout Utah. The Joe Hill matter was well covered by the *Herald* and the *Telegram*. We now have available to us online census records through *Ancestry.com*. We have LDS church records that are more available now than they were before. The most underused resource is the legal database of appellate decisions called *Westlaw*. *Westlaw* has all decisions from every jurisdiction beginning in the nineteenth century. This allows us to track the careers and moves of the lawyers involved in the case.

We have firsthand reports of some of the events, particularly from Elizabeth Gurley Flynn and Bill Haywood. There are miscellaneous records of Utah lawyers, including *The History of the Bar and Bench of Utah,* published in 1913. There is also *Pioneers and Prominent Men* by Frank Eshom, which came out in 1913. There is the biography of Justice Straup in the *Bar Journal* and other miscellaneous books.

This project has consumed two years of time. My nephew, Eric Lougee, spent the better part of a year taking me to used bookstores, where I purchased strangely titled histories. I have written and rewritten. My colleagues have read the various versions as they have come off the word processor. My wife and children have humored me in the search of Joe Hill materials. To all I owe thanks.

When I returned to Utah, my friend Dr. Mike Nelson, of the University of Utah, took me to lunch. He took me by Sugarhouse Park. I had seen pictures of the Mormon polygamists at the state penitentiary, but I never realized that the prison was within the city boundaries. Nothing is left except mounds and uneven terrain. As I later thought of the prison, I came to realize that Utah actually shot Joe Hill in an urban setting. This is but one more incongruity in this long and sad story.

Oh Say what is Truth

Yes, say what is truth? Tis the brightest prize
To which mortals or Gods can aspire
Go search in the depths where it glittering lies.
Or ascend in pursuit to the loftiest skies
Tis an aim for the noblest desire.

Then, say what is truth? Tis the last and the first,
For the limits of time it steps o'er,
Tho the heavens depart and the earth's fountains burst,
Truth, the sum of existence will weather the worst,
Eternal, unchanged, evermore.

John Jaques
(1827–1900)
Latter-day Saint Hymn 272
Formerly printed in the Mormon Scripture Pearl of Great Price

Chapter 1

A Citizen of the Universe

A page of history is worth a pound of logic.

Justice Oliver Wendell Holmes

I

A Saint Paul Hardware Store

When he was arrested in Utah and accused of murder, the authorities asked Joe Hill where he was from. He said, "I'm a citizen of the universe." In his songs, Joe Hill clearly saw himself as a member of the laboring class who knew no nationality. People were not divided into Swedes, Germans, and Americans, but bosses and labor. It did not matter where he came from. All that mattered was that he was a member of labor.

There are some factual matters that can be shown without dispute. He was born in Sweden. His life in Sweden was without much controversy. He was raised in a typical middle-class Swedish home. When his father died, his family broke up. He came to the United States in 1902, probably with a brother. He was never naturalized a citizen. We think he was probably in San Francisco during the 1906 earthquake, because there was a letter that came from there addressed to his local hometown newspaper. In 1910, Hill joined the Industrial Workers of the World (IWW) in San Pedro, California. (He consistently uses his Union local number in his songs. In

Casey Jones the Union Scab we find "Angels Union 23.") We do know he was in California in the fall of 1913.

Surprisingly, Joseph Hillstrom was found in the 1910 census. He was living in Saint Paul, Minnesota. He was single and resided in a boarding house. The birth date is right. He was born in Sweden. The only information the census taker possibly recorded incorrectly was the date of emigration, which was recorded as 1897. It may disappoint the followers of the Joe Hill legend to know that he worked in a hardware store.

Looking at his songs, one might expect that he traveled the continent. He wrote songs about strikes in British Columbia, Massachusetts, New Jersey, California, and probably Washington State. Outside of the songs and the 1910 census, there is no evidence that he left the west coast. It is claimed that he worked at the mines in Park City. It is also claimed that he was part of a group that invaded Mexico. His documented labor history is limited. According to Bill Haywood, the IWW general secretary, the only time Joe Hill met the labor leader was in a 1913 free speech movement at San Diego.

There is much about his life that is mysterious or even ominous. When Joe Hill was committed to the Utah State Penitentiary, he had two other unaccounted for gunshot wounds. Where or how he was shot remains unknown. How he supported himself and where he obtained money is unknown. In his letter to the board of pardons, Hill said, "Being aware that my past record has nothing to do with the facts of this case, I will not dwell upon the subject beyond saying that I have worked all my life as a mechanic and at times as a musician."

Joe Hill is most interesting because his first language was, of course, Swedish. He wrote numerous songs for the labor movement, particularly for the IWW, in English, and the songs are brilliant propaganda. Joe Hill could take melodies that were known to the American laboring class and write words that explained the union doctrine in terms that could not be misunderstood. Even today, one cannot miss the parody and puns on words. His work is clever and even fun.

But beyond that, while Joe Hill was in jail in Salt Lake City, he wrote a long letter to the editor of the *Salt Lake Telegram*. His English prose is outstanding. It is clear. The grammar is correct. It is what one would expect of a college upperclassman who has taken the standard writing classes. There is no indication of what person, if anyone, tutored Joe Hill in English. The probable explanation is that Joe Hill was a self-tutored linguistic genius. In any event, Joe Hill's ability to communicate with the labor movement in both prose and poetry was unmatched by his contemporaries.

II

Weird and Vague

Given its notoriety and importance to the labor movement, the facts of the crime for which Joe Hill was executed are surprisingly sparse. He was accused of the murder of a former policeman named Morrison who owned a grocery store in south Salt Lake. Morrison's son was also killed in the incident.[9]

On the night of January 10, 1914, two presumed robbers came into the grocery. They had bandanas over their faces, and they immediately opened fire with .38 caliber revolvers. They fired six times.[10] Morrison and his oldest son were shot and killed. Morrison had a younger son who was twelve at the time. This boy hid in the back of the store. This young boy was the only real witness to the crime, although there were other people who testified that a person resembling Joe Hill was in the vicinity of the store. Morrison was scared of robbers coming into his grocery store. He had a loaded weapon, which was also a .38 caliber revolver. No witness, including the younger son, heard the Morrison gun fired during the robbery.

After the assault was over, the authorities found the Morrison gun just outside the reach of the older son's body with one chamber discharged. There was a path of blood that led away from the store. There was a witness who said she saw a man who was groaning.

Two hours later, Joe Hill showed up at a doctor's office in Murray with a serious bullet wound through his chest. The doctor was a socialist, which is probably why Joe Hill picked him. A second doctor showed up and assisted in Hill's care. Health care was not what we would have expected in our day. People were a lot stronger in those days, and after the doctors patched Joe Hill's wounds, they took him to the home where he was staying. (This was a family of Swedish immigrants. The local press reported that Hill had known two of the brothers while in San Pedro. It is not demonstrably known if Hill knew the family from his youth in Sweden.)

When the doctors were treating him, they saw that Joe Hill had a weapon in a shoulder harness that fell out. The doctor who took Joe Hill home was driving a Model T. The car sputtered and stopped. When the car stopped, Joe Hill threw away his gun. The doctors asked him where and how he was shot. Joe Hill told the story that he repeated over and over again, that he was shot by an unknown man in a fight over an unknown woman at an unknown place. Chief Justice Straup would later describe this alibi as "weird and vague." Joe Hill was arrested. There never was a witness who positively identified him at the scene. If this crime happened today, the authorities would do a DNA test of the blood trail, and there would not have been an argument over guilt or innocence.

With respect to the eyewitnesses, we know their testimony is inherently unreliable. We had a case from the Utah Supreme Court in 2009 in which Justice Durham said it was an error to exclude the testimony of an expert who would opine that eyewitness testimony is not reliable.[11]

People can and have told stories embellishing those facts. That is part of the difficulty in the explanation of the Joe Hill case. Simply put, there are many holes in the story that can never be known. The worst offender in historical fabrication was Wallace Stegner. He calls his book, originally titled *The Preacher and the Slave,* an autobiographical novel. In it he freely invents characters and conversations, all leading to his conclusion that Joe Hill was guilty. Stegner tries to cover his offenses by calling his work fictional, but he was clearly intending to weigh in on the Joe Hill controversy.

The most factual account of Hill's pre-Utah life is Gibbs Smith's book *Joe Hill*. Not even Smith explains the missing years of Joe Hill's life in America. Joe Hill intentionally left his life a mystery. The best that can be done is to document the few times he can be pinned to factual circumstances, which are scarce prior to his arrest. In my mind, this mysterious background adds greatly to the Joe Hill mystic. People can and do make assumptions. Those who believe in his guilt assume he led a life of crime. Those who believe he was a labor hero assume he was an ordinary workingman. Working in a Saint Paul hardware store is probably disappointing to both groups.

I am a little reluctant to discuss the facts of the Morrison murders. There are two groups of people reading this book. Those under the age of forty have never heard of Joe Hill, because Joe Hill isn't taught in the Utah public schools, and that is in both junior high and high school. Even in Professor Dean May's college text for Utah History, Dr. May gives Joe Hill two lines. (Wisely, Dr. May does not opine on guilt or innocence.)

The other group reading this book constitutes Joe Hill aficionados. It is very difficult to write for Joe Hill aficionados because they know all the facts. For example, I wrote a preliminary article that I submitted to *Utah Historical Quarterly*. I was speaking specifically about the trial and the appeal. I limited myself to facts that appeared in the legal record.

I recited the facts as Chief Justice Straup[12] outlined them in his appellate opinion. I wrote, "Joe Hill threw away his gun." I got back a comment with three bold underlines that said, "It was a Luger." Well, Justice Straup didn't say, "Luger." He said, "Gun." In fact, if you want to be accurate, the only testimony that came before the jury or the court was that the doctor who saw Joe Hill's weapon thought it looked like a Colt automatic. But in his letter to the newspaper, Joe Hill said he had a Luger, so everyone who is presumed to know anything about the case "knows" that Joe Hill had a Luger.

There are all kinds of other "knowledge" similar to the presumption that Joe Hill carried a Luger. A student reportedly wrote a paper on the Joe Hill case. Joe Hill's wound came into his body in a unique manner. It came in and went out his coat at an upward angle. It clearly went through his body. The authorities never found the bullet. This student reportedly

5

opined on why the authorities did not find the bullet. His explanation was, the bullet was in the ceiling, and the authorities never looked there. You can't argue with such logic. You certainly cannot argue with such "facts."

Other people have written about evidence that cannot be proven. Leading away from the robbery scene, the authorities recovered some blood. The state chemist testified it was mammalian blood. Some of the people who have written on the case said, "That means that they couldn't tell it was human." When you read three or four murder cases from the time period, you find that the same chemist testifies every time, and he testifies the same way. You realize all of a sudden that's the state of the art. The testimony that the blood was mammalian would have been persuasive in an era that did not know about blood typing.

Perhaps it is my training and experience as a trial lawyer, but I remain suspicious of recitation of "facts" and inferences beyond the basic information found in the trial testimony, the appellate opinions, and contemporary news accounts.

While it is impossible to learn more "facts" about the crime, there is much to be discovered about the trial and the events in Utah. Those events are actually well documented and perhaps tell more about Joe Hill than we would learn from speculation over his past and the events of the murder.

III

Axel Steele and the IWW

There is one matter that may be resolved with absolute certainty. In the disbarment of Judge Hilton, Chief Justice Straup says that the terms "Industrial Workers of the World" and "IWW" never appeared in the Joe Hill trial transcript. Likewise, they never appeared in any of the briefs filed on Hill's behalf in the Utah Supreme Court. The first time anyone referred to the union was in the commutation hearing. This is surprising, as thousands of individual Union members would later protest the conviction. In Governor Spry's Hillstrom file (found in the *Utah Digital*

Archives) there are several thousand letters written by Union supporters in the attempt to save Joe Hill's life.

Mostly relying upon IWW newspapers, Professor Foner gives the impression that Hill's union connection was at issue from the beginning. No one told the people in Utah. The argument that the Joe Hill trial had something to do with the labor movement is made by Foner and playwright Barrie Stavis. They placed great trust in the IWW and socialist press. In my mind, their reliance upon *Solidarity* is misguided. Most of the information is second and third hand. More importantly, the Salt Lake jury pool was not reading the IWW material but was reading the Salt Lake City press. There are significant differences between the events reported in *Solidarity* and the *Industrial Worker* and those found in the Salt Lake press.

Dr. Foner attempts to demonstrate a particularly fierce anti-union sentiment in Salt Lake City. He cites as evidence the June 1913 IWW strike against the Utah Construction Company in Tucker, Utah. The company was putting a new rail line for the Southern Pacific through Spanish Fork Canyon. The IWW was believed to have struck for a twenty-five cent an hour raise. They supposedly forced this wage raise from the company.[13] This strike was barely mentioned in the Salt Lake press. The *Herald* reported on June 12, 1913, that a force of ten guards under former Chief Deputy Axel Steele of the Salt Lake County sheriff's office was sent to guard the mouth of the canyon.[14] There was slight notice given this alleged strike in Utah other than two articles in Carbon County. Indeed, the Carbon County press was not even certain that the IWW had in fact struck the company. It is certain that if the strike did occur, it did not last longer than one week.

Foner cites an account from a labor newspaper, the *Industrial Worker*, published in 1945, to support the notion that there was ongoing bad blood between the IWW and the Utah Construction Company during the summer of 1913. He argues that this bad blood led to a climate of hate in Salt Lake City against the IWW. Foner believes that there were numerous antiunion actions. There is very little contemporary evidence in support of this proposition in the Salt Lake press.

Foner primarily bases his allegation on the supposed hostility of hired Utah Construction Company guards to the IWW in Salt Lake City. In particular, he claims that Axel Steele [15] was in charge of intimidating the union after the strike. Prior to 1912, Steele showed up regularly in the Salt Lake press as a member of the police force. His experience as a guard in strike-related episodes was actually quite limited. He took a detachment of deputies to Bingham Canyon in 1912. This is the only confirmed allegation of Axel Steele involved in strike work before the Tucker incident. [16]

The *Salt Lake Herald* reports a riot occurring on August 8, 1913. An IWW organizer, James F. Morgan, had been imprisoned for thirty days in Utah County over some incident in the Tucker Strike. Upon his release, he spoke at a Salt Lake City street meeting. He denounced not only the Utah Construction Company but also the American flag. Listening in a nearby bar, Axel Steele decided to cause trouble. He waded into the crowd with a small American flag, followed by four of his accomplices. This insult was too much for an armed IWW follower, Tom Murphy, who opened fire. Steele was shot in the hip but protected by a thick wallet. Three other followers of Steele were also shot. The only casualties on the IWW side were bruises. The police were not able to restore order. The fisticuffs continued until the fire department used its hoses on the men.

This is the only violent incident involving either Axel Steele or James Morgan recorded in 1913 in the *Salt Lake Herald* or the *Telegram*. [17] Outside of Salt Lake, the story got little play even in Carbon County, the site of the supposed strike. [18] The press stories are inconsistent about injuries to the IWW speaker. In one version, Morgan was significantly beaten. This was contradicted by Morgan, who denied personal injury. [19]

Whatever charge was laid against James Morgan, he was not in jail long. On September 4, 1913, he gave an interview to the *Herald*. Morgan denied that the IWW was going to fill the Salt Lake City jail because "We have not been hurt and we have not been denied permission to hold our street meetings." He denied making any threat against the authorities. [20] Within days thereafter, Morgan had moved on to Ogden. [21]

If Salt Lake City was unalterably prejudiced against the IWW, the actions of the city fathers were very strange. Foner stated that the *Deseret News* published anti-IWW material the second week of March 1914 and that this was an attempt to prejudice the jury. Again, the truth is not as simple as Foner represents. This is shown by an article published by the *Salt Lake Telegram* on March 23, 1914. At that time, a large number of IWW members passed through Salt Lake City on their way to a free speech fight in Denver. There was no free speech fight in Salt Lake City in spring 1914. The presence of the union men had nothing to do with Joe Hill. In fact, there is no mention in the press indicating that the traveling IWW members even knew Joe Hill was in jail on a murder charge.

Rather than harass the unemployed army, Police Chief B. F. Grant[22] made arrangements to feed the men at a Salt Lake City restaurant. The restaurant agreed to give the men all they could eat for twenty-five cents. The police chief visited their camp. "When I was informed that a part of the Kelly army of unemployed men which had been causing considerable trouble in California had arrived in Salt Lake, I anticipated a greater difficulty in handling them than I have experienced with the hundred or more men who arrived this morning . . . I found the men to be more like gentlemen in stringent circumstances than an army of bully agitators who preferred trouble than work."[23]

Foner's conclusion that Joe Hill was convicted on the strength of his connection to the IWW is hard to sustain. The first half of the trial transcript had disappeared long before Foner wrote his book. Justice Straup is unimpeachable in his representation that Hill's IWW membership had never come before the Utah courts. There is no mention of IWW membership in the Utah press. The *Telegram* had a reporter in all sessions of the trial, and they do not mention IWW membership at the trial.[24]

Foner and to a lesser extent Barrie Stavis are left with the argument that the jury assimilated knowledge and prejudice by osmosis. Their arguments simply are not supported by the existing record. Believing him innocent based solely on status as a workingman, they reach conclusions about the Salt Lake community that are perhaps unwise in retrospect. In sum, neither the unknown facts of Hill's prior life nor the sketchy facts of the crime are sufficient to judge the matter. The argument that Salt Lake City was unduly prejudiced does not stand up to close examination. Explanation for the accusation, trial, and conviction must be found elsewhere.

IV

Rae Wellman's First Trial

Early in the murder trial, the city editor of the *Salt Lake Telegram* sent a new reporter to view the afternoon session of the Joe Hill trial.[25] This was, in fact, Rae Wellman's first time visiting a courtroom. She misunderstood some of the details of the trial. She thought the gun in evidence actually belonged to Joe Hill when it was only an example of a handgun shown the doctors. The surviving son, Merlin Morrison's, name is misspelled. But this is the only real-life view we have inside the courtroom.

> The day was a dead hot one and the small courtroom reeked in the acrid odor of some fifty men sweltering in their heavy clothes.

> Twelve jurors, one judge, three lawyers, one clerk, one court reporter, two men with duties not discoverable by me—and the prisoner. Twenty men to try one man for his life. Twenty men weaving intricately the threads of law and justice into life or death for a fellow man. The law is indeed a grand and awesome thing.

The trial had all of the forms of evidence one would expect in a precomputer trial. There were diagrams of the blood trail traced and retraced on a "blackboard map." Joe Hill's clothing was offered into evidence. She describes Judge Ritchie as "little more than the blur of a thin nervous face from whose mouth issued from time to time soft and whimsically spoken words of advice or admonition."

It is her description of Joe Hill that fascinates. She says that Hill "glanced indifferently" at the material evidence. "He did listen very carefully to the remarkably clear and direct testimony of young Berlin (*sic*) Morrison . . . the prisoner's habitually shifting glances—yet not more so than the judge or the jurors or the lawyers—fixed on the pale, fat face of this young but most important witness against him. I imagined, or was it so, that he was feeling an intense enmity for this boy ..."

Physically Joe Hill was "rugged, seasoned, handsome in a virile way." She thought him fascinated by the fight: "the biggest in his experience of adventurous living—even though the stakes be his life and the odds against him."

We are indebted to Rae Wellman, for this is the only description of Joe Hill at the trial. We are left to wonder at her description of a look of enmity at the Morrison boy. As we shall see, Joe Hill would lose his emotional equilibrium over the way his lawyers questioned the boy, who, after all, was thirteen.

Chapter 2

The Little Red Songbook

Many ideas grow better when transplanted into another mind than
the one they sprung up.

Justice Oliver Wendell Holmes

I

The Bravery of Vincent St. John

In 1952, while Elizabeth Gurley Flynn was tried and sentenced for
violating the Smith Act, she wrote the history of her early labor agitation.
The Smith Act was aimed at the leadership of the American Communist
Party. By 1952, Miss Flynn had been an active communist for thirty years.
Among her earlier activities, she was a cofounder of the American Civil
Liberties Union. In the shadow of a prison sentence, she went back fifty
years to her activities as an organizer for the Industrial Workers of the
World. Particularly, she remembered her old friend Vincent St. John.[26]

"I never met a man that I admired more than Vincent St. John. He was
a fabulous figure who had come out of the class struggle of the West."
St. John was only thirty years old in 1907 when he became the general
organizer of the IWW. Miss Flynn describes him as short and slight in
build, though broad shouldered, quick, and graceful in his movements.

"Quiet, self contained, modest but his keenness of mind and (could) outmatch any opponent."

Miss Flynn describes St. John's early life. His father was an express rider who lost an arm fighting Indians. Vincent St. John went to work at age eighteen for the Bisbee (Arizona) Copper Company. At age twenty-four, he was president of the Western Federation of Miners local in Telluride, Colorado. In 1901, there was a massive strike in Telluride. One of the mine owners, Arthur Collins, organized a "Citizen's Alliance" to oppose the strike. Collins was murdered by shotgun. St. John, as president of the union, was charged with murder and defended by Judge Orin Hilton, who would later play an important role in the Joe Hill case. In fact, Miss Flynn quotes Judge Hilton as saying that he defended Vincent St. John in a dozen murder cases that never came to trial.

St. John was known to be a fearless organizer. Miss Flynn quotes a company detective as saying that St. John had caused more trouble in the Colorado mines than any twenty other men. He organized in the Coeur d'Alene, Idaho, district as well as Colorado. He often used assumed names for personal protection.

After the formation of the IWW, St. John became its chief organizer. His signal success was in Goldfield, Nevada. This mining camp was once bustling but now is a ghost town. St. John not only organized the miners but also the town workers. The mine owners engineered a jurisdictional fight between the American Federation of Labor and the Western Federation of Miners, which was affiliated with the IWW. St. John almost lost his life (and did lose the use of a hand) when shot by a labor rival. He ultimately was rescued by friends and sent to hospital in Chicago.

The miners loved St. John for more than his union skills. St. John led a rescue party in a Telluride disaster that saved many miners' lives. He lived thereafter with chronic bronchial asthma, which was believed to lead to his early death.

In 1915, St. John, worn out by union struggles, left the leadership and even the union itself to prospect in New Mexico. This did not save him from the roundup of IWW leaders in 1919. He was convicted, along with most of the leadership, of conspiracy. Judge Kennesaw Mountain Landis sentenced him to a long prison term and a $20,000 fine. St. John served time in Leavenworth Prison until pardoned by President Harding. He died in 1929 in San Francisco, almost unremembered. Years later, friends, including Elizabeth Gurley Flynn, erected a small monument to his memory.

St. John was thought of as a "dynamiter" and a murderous criminal. The truth was that even though personally fearless in labor organization, St. John was a married man with mild habits. Only framed conspiracy charges sullied his civic record.

II

What the IWW Believed

In 1917, Red Dawn Press of Cincinnati published a small book or extended pamphlet by St. John entitled *The IWW: Its History, Structure, and Methods.* It is a very serious work, containing the history of conventions, dissent, and strikes won and lost. The importance of the book comes only with careful reading about assumptions and intent. Vincent St. John explicitly sets out the worldview of the members of the IWW.

Writers have often quoted the IWW preamble, which states that "the working class and the employing class have nothing in common. There can be no peace so long as hunger and want are found among millions of working people and the few who make up the employing class, have all the good things of life." St. John explained this position with exactness. "There is but one bargain that the IWW will make with the employing class—*complete surrender of all control of industry to the organized workers.*"

What is not commonly understood is that the IWW leadership had much in common with the Luddites of industrializing England. Both sought to protect the rights of labor from increased mechanization. To the IWW, modern mechanism would destroy the livelihoods of all skilled labor. St. John could not envision a middle class of educated and skilled workers necessary to feed a modern economy. He believed that machinery would reduce all workers to unskilled labor. Thus, instead of economic and social classes coming together, they were growing further apart, and without organization, the employing class would inevitably win any contest.

St. John believed that the world's resources were limited in an almost Malthusian manner. Therefore, the contest between classes was over an ever-diminishing resource base.

The IWW was Marxist in the sense that they saw coming class revolution. Taking some elements from the anarchists, they saw post-revolution industrial concerns being managed by the collective wisdom and votes of the workers themselves. Indeed, in their wars with the various socialist parties, they make plain that they reject coercive government.

All government (including government by socialists) was merely the tool of the employers. St. John trusted no one, including courts and local or national government. All would act in the interests of the bosses.
St. John states that in this contest between workers and bosses, the IWW is "not concerned with right and wrong." "It aims to use any and all tactics that will get the result sought with the least expenditure of time and energy." What Vincent St. John meant by these words is uncertain. In his own life, he organized labor, led strikes, and demanded response from the bosses. He was frustrating to confront. But he never murdered anyone. In that light, St. John must be taken to mean that labor could and should use any legitimate tool at hand to enforce their demands.

St. John is very explicit about the tools to be used in the labor struggle. Since any agreement with an employer was temporary, no contracts would be signed with an employer. If a contract was signed, it would be violated as soon as the union found itself in an advantageous position. The union might strike but only when in an advantageous position. A short strike might be better than a long one, because the workers would be back on the job before they could be replaced. Then when the workers felt strong enough, they would strike again.

St. John discusses the union's use of free speech movements. Beginning in Spokane, Washington, the union fought the authorities' ability to keep them from proselytizing on street corners. When the city fathers passed a law against speaking for the union in public, the union simply had enough members arrested to overflow the jails. They repeated this tactic to much success throughout the west. Joe Hill was a participant in the California free speech fights.

There was also sabotage. St. John found sabotage a tactic to force concessions from the employers. Because there would be an ever-growing army of unemployed as the world industrialized, the IWW "aims to establish the shorter work day, and to slow up the working pace, thus compelling the employment of more and more workers."[27] It is not clear what sabotage meant beyond St. John's description. The union had a sign—a black cat—that signified sabotage. In practice, it usually meant exactly what St. John said it meant—wasting time on the job.

The employing class was the main enemy. But the IWW also stood against "trade" or "craft" unionism. The collection of craft unions collected in the American Federation of Labor ignored the fact that all labor would be reduced to the unskilled. Further, craft unionists saw their issues as aligned with the "bosses." They were therefore a deadly enemy to be fought at every opportunity.

St. John was equally adamant about the dangers of other organizations on the left. There were two classes of socialist politicians: Marxist "impossibilists" and opportune reformers. There were "labor union fakirs" who sought to take the new union off of its revolutionary path. Finally, there were the anarchists—a group that caused St. John the least trouble

With this collection of enemies, it is not difficult to see why the IWW did not endure. It was hopelessly romantic. The union even organized a local for rodeo cowboys. It celebrated the individual at the sacrifice of the organization. The body of IWW members, popularly known as "Wobblies," would never have accepted the discipline demanded by the communists. In order to achieve a mass movement, dues were minimal. This meant that the union was never able to sustain a strike without outside help. Indeed, St. John claimed that a protracted strike really meant that the union had not properly evaluated the situation.

The union suffered incredible persecution. At the beginning of World War I, a "Citizens Alliance" deported every IWW member, supporter, and suspect person from Bisbee, Arizona. The authorities simply put everyone on a train, ran it to the New Mexico border, and abandoned the men without food or water. Elizabeth Gurley Flynn's associate, Floyd Little, was lynched in Butte, Montana. After the end of the war, there was a riot at Centralia, Washington, in which an IWW member and veteran was tortured and lynched.

In the second administration of Woodrow Wilson, the lawyers (as well as the historians) took leave of their senses on civil liberties. Attorney General Palmer became convinced that this union of individualists, dynamiters, and "sabotage" was dangerous to the nation. The federal government and numerous states passed "criminal syndicalism" laws aimed at the union. There were mass arrests throughout the West. The government attempted to put an end to the union by arresting and trying the leadership in Chicago in 1919. Bill Haywood, the union general secretary, badly misread the national mood and legal atmosphere. He ordered the leadership to show up and with utter disregard of the realities, refused to put on a defense. The union leadership was convicted. This was a blow from which the IWW never recovered, although its fighting mentality was later resurrected in the CIO.

III

The Progressive Response to the IWW

With its extensive list of enemies, it is not surprising that the union did not recognize its most dangerous foe. The union's strongest period was in the era of the progressive movement, and progressives, both Democratic and Republican, wanted change. In particular, they were tired of the excesses of business at the cost of the public good. They were also tired of the excesses of labor in resisting business. In short, they wanted labor peace for the good of the nation. The progressive attitude toward the IWW was most succinctly stated by the progressive president Theodore Roosevelt when he called them "undesirable citizens."

The progressives were militantly middle class. In foreseeing the rise of the American middle class, the progressives were on the right side of history. The IWW, with its quaint notions of a shrinking economy in which all workers were unskilled, turned out to be wrong. The IWW did not foresee the vast expansion of education and the possibilities it would offer the American economy over the course of the century. St. John, being self-educated, could not imagine sons of working men attending college. He could not imagine the "craft" unions delivering a middle-class lifestyle to their members.

It is not that history inevitably picks winners and losers. The country was well on its way to middle-class respectability when the IWW was formed. The IWW's failure was not in its inability to peer into the distant future. It was a failure to appreciate the events of the immediate past and seek out allies who were equally dedicated to limiting the power of the trusts and monopolies.

By the time of the Joe Hill trial, the progressives had achieved their major goals in curtailing the economic power of the "trusts." Theodore Roosevelt had shown the power of the bully pulpit. His administration brought anti-trust actions, resolved the coal strike, and curtailed the unfettered power of the trusts through effective threats. By 1913 the constitution had been amended to allow the graduated income tax. This was a popular progressive policy deemed necessary to make the employer class pay its fair share for government. In 1913, the constitution was also amended to provide for the direct election of senators, thus taking the power from state legislatures that too often were dominated by the property-owning class. In 1913, the progressives also established the Federal Reserve. This was believed to be a method of controlling wide swings in the economy. Even progressive intellectualism made strides in 1913. Charles Beard, a supporter of progressive causes, published his *Economic Interpretation of the Constitution of the United States*. Beard, of course, argued that the government was founded by economic elites, and with his focus on the present, argued for curtailment of economic favor.

John Graham Brooks gave the progressive reply to the challenge of the IWW in his 1913 book *American Syndicalism; the IWW.* John Graham Brooks (1846–1938) was a native of New Hampshire. He attended

Oberlin College from 1869 to 1871 and graduated from Harvard Divinity School in 1875. He was an ordained Unitarian minister who took an interest in labor affairs. He organized classes for working men. He lectured on labor at Harvard and for many years investigated strikes for the department of labor. He traveled extensively in Europe and was familiar with labor thought on the continent. He was the first president of the National Consumers' League and president of the American Social Science Association in 1904. He lectured widely on labor issues.

To Brooks, the IWW correctly identified the nature of the conflict between labor and the employers. However, the IWW tactics were wasteful. "[T]he defiant riotous ways of this American Syndicalism are past understanding." Sabotage was designed to allow men to hold on to their jobs while effactually going on strike. Brooks tells the story of men on strike whose replacements were inefficient. The strikers learned the lesson of not having to produce any faster than the replacements. So under the name of sabotage, they purposely slowed down. Brooks gives another example. One machine broke, and four thousand men stopped working. Again, this was sabotage.

Brooks was highly offended at the IWW notion that only labor contributed to industrial output. Brooks recognized, if the IWW did not, that capital investment was necessary for any major enterprise.

The major focus of the progressive movement's labor policy was to bring peace to relationships in the name of more production and better living standards. Brooks simply could not accept the notion that labor could refuse to cooperate in increasing output. Essentially, Brooks was calling for an adult conversation between labor and management in the interests of the community.

IV

Joe Hill as an Intellectual

Brooks was an intellectual studying labor and management as a student. Such intellectuals were few in the labor movement. Richard Hofstadter in *Anti-Intellectualism in America* noted that even in the craft unions, intellectuals became prominent only when those unions took on the attributes of business. College men were suspect because they did not come up through the ranks and therefore did not have the experience of actually working in the trade. While the IWW leadership included many intelligent men and women, some of whom were self-educated, they rejected the intellectualism of their socialist counterparts.

The IWW established a number of newspapers, printing in several languages. Besides St. John's book, there are only two books in common circulation discussing the intellectual thought of the leadership of the IWW. One was by Bill Haywood (*Bill Haywood's Book*). The other was Elizabeth Gurley Flynn's *Rebel Girl.*

Haywood's book is self-congratulatory. It might have been entitled, *"How I Was the Labor Movement in America."* It barely mentions Vincent St. John, who kept industrial unionism together for difficult periods, including the time Haywood was in prison. Haywood has an interesting life, but the book is hardly a balanced treatment of the labor movement. It closes with Haywood in Russia meeting Lenin. Lenin assures Haywood that the workers controlled the revolution in the Soviet Union. One can hardly imagine the rank and file of the IWW submitting to communist discipline. The Soviets published the book to establish their own legitimacy in the American labor movement. Haywood, presumably, had forgotten that the IWW rejected all government and most assuredly rejected government that coerced the governed.

Flynn's book was written years after she had left the IWW in a dispute with Haywood. It is a somewhat run-on collection of incident after incident in a very full life. Her perspective was that of a union organizer involved with day-to-day agitation. It was written years after she had accepted the discipline of the International Communist Party, and it is written through the eyes of a dedicated communist. Looking back, she viewed her IWW period as a "period of ideological and organizational confusion." The IWW was mistaken to abandon politics. As the working class had to capture political power after the revolution, it was a mistake to rely upon the union. Private violence and governmental persecution turned the union into a legal defense fund. "Rank and filism" made it impossible to control industrial action. Still, she saw the IWW as sowing class consciousness and industrial unionism far and wide.[28]

Haywood, St. John, and Flynn were not contemplative figures. They had a union to run under very difficult circumstances. Haywood and Flynn later had difficulty comprehending the subtleties of communist doctrine. It is true that they were inspirational speakers and could explain the immediate needs of the movement to their followers. They did not have the power of imaginative language. They were not poets.

Joe Hill, on the other hand, was an intellectual. Hofstadter said that wit was the sign of an intellectual. Joe Hill demonstrated both wit and powerful poetic language that resonated then and continues to resonate within the labor movement. This is perhaps the secret of Joe Hill's continuing vitality. It is the reason a poor Swedish immigrant became the cause of the nation and one reason why this debate has meaning today.

This gift of creativity was where Joe Hill showed his superiority in explaining the goals and doctrine of the union. The union had problems with "craft" workers not supporting their strikes. The AFL often ignored IWW strikes and in many instances took the position of the employer. It was a common problem denounced by the IWW leadership.

Joe Hill explained the problem to the workers in terms they understood. He wrote *Casey Jones the Union Scab.* "Scabbing" was the pejorative term for strike breaking. The legendary engineer refused to help the workers win the strike with the Southern Pacific. He kept running his engine to spite the strikers. Because of the strike, Casey Jones ran his train into the water, where he died. Joe Hill has Casey Jones "scabbing on the angels" until Saint Peter sends him to hell for scabbing. No one could mistake what Hill was saying.

The IWW was at war with the American Federation of Labor and its president, Samuel Gompers, over the organization of unskilled workers. Joe Hill wrote *Mr. Block.*

> Block hiked back to the city, but wasn't doing well.
> He said, "I'll join the union—the great AF of L."

He got a job next morning, got fired in the night,
He said, "I'll see Sam Gompers and he'll fix that foreman
right."
Sam Gompers said, "You see,
You've got our sympathy."

Hill wrote songs about union busting in Lawrence, Massachusetts. He wrote songs about unionizing workers on the Canadian Pacific Railroad. He encouraged the organization.

Everybody's joining it, joining what, joining it!
Everybody's joining it, joining what, joining it!
One Big Union, that's the workers' choice,
One Big Union, that's the only noise,
One Big Union, shout with all your voice.

The Boss is feeling mighty blue,
He don't know just what to do
We have got his goat, got him by the throat,
Soon he'll work or go starving
Join IWW,
Don't let bosses trouble you,
Come join with us—everybody does—
You've got nothing to lose.

Where the organizers conceived a world where the workers received the fruits of industrialization, Hill wrote *Workers of the World, Awaken*. Note how Hill echoes Vincent St. John's statements that there is no concept of right or wrong in dealing with the employing class.

Workers of the World Awaken,
 Break your chains, demand your rights.
All the wealth you make is taken
 By exploiting parasites.
Shall you kneel in deep submission?
 From your cradles to your graves?
Is the height of your ambition
 To be good and willing slaves?

Arise, ye prisoners of starvation!
Fight for your own emancipation;
Arise, ye slaves of every nation.
 In one Union grand.
Our little ones for bread are crying,
And millions are from hunger dying,
The end the means is justifying
'Tis the final stand.

Besides his vivid images, Joe Hill was a powerful wordsmith. In *Preacher and the Slave,* he introduced the term "Pie in the Sky" to the English language.

Bill Haywood and the other IWW leaders recognized Hill's importance to the movement. Although Haywood and Hill met only once in San Diego, Haywood said that "[A]ll of Joe Hill's songs breathe the class struggle and are fine propaganda."[29] Most of Hill's songs were published in the IWW's *Little Red Songbook.* This collection of labor songs has remained in print.

It is true that Joe Hill never held an official position in the union. When Utah executed him, they shot the most effective statesmen of IWW goals. All of the union members knew of Hill's work. They continually sang his songs. They were encouraged by his industrial vision, which explained the union's goals and positions to the illiterate in terms easily understood. Shooting Hill was not an attempt to decapitate the union as were the other conspiracy trials. On the other hand, it was a direct strike at the beliefs of the union members.

Chapter 3

A Most Dangerous Game

The only price much cared for by the powerful is power.

Justice Oliver Wendell Holmes

Propaganda or Law

The court system in the age of American industrialism was reactionary. Defenders of the status quo used the courts to sustain their notions of property rights. They found comfort in the received beliefs that the constitution protected them against legitimate labor demands. There never was a strike in the era that was not met by an injunction against organization by a federal court. Beyond injunctions, the court system was used to decapitate union leadership and intimidate the rank and file. Arbitrary arrests were common. The organizer Elizabeth Gurley Flynn said in a melancholic voice, "I got arrested again."

The truth was that there were two games in play in labor trials. There was the legal game played out against the backdrop of a supposed commitment to the rule of law. Equally important was the propaganda game of the labor movement. It is clear that propaganda was as important as winning the criminal case. For example, the labor movement invested much time and effort in the defense of the McNamara brothers who were accused of bombing the *Los Angeles Times*. The labor defense machine was

24

fully engaged when Clarence Darrow pled the brothers guilty to avoid execution. The reaction to this propaganda defeat was such that Darrow never did another labor case.

The stakes of this dual game were well understood by the progressive labor writer John Graham Brooks writing about the murder trial arising out of the IWW strike in Lawrence, Massachusetts:

> If it is the express object to multiply the agitators' power over labor, not twice or thrice but twenty times it is easily done ... let (citizens' anxiety) act in heat and with suspicious disregard for justice and at one a hundred new avenues of influence are open to men like Ettor and Giovannitti. If they had gone to the electric chair, the incensed imagination of millions of workingmen and women would have crowned them martyrs. Solemn hours would have been set apart to do them honor and the place of their burial would have been a shrine.[30]

Brooks goes on to argue that the fact of his arrest gave Ettor an audience that he would not otherwise have gained. "Their lightest word has significance and carrying power that make the jail the shortest, quickest way to influence."

As Gurley Flynn noted, the continuous arrests turned the IWW into a criminal defense organization. Even the participants themselves had trouble distinguishing between legal defense and propaganda.

In the Joe Hill case, it is hard to distinguish between legal maneuvers and propaganda. Certainly, the trial lawyers, although socialists, thought they were defending the case as a legal matter. Their politics showed throughout, which did not help in their defense because Ernest MacDougall took the opportunity to make socialist speeches. After conviction, it is obviously the propaganda perpetuated by Judge Hilton and not the application of the law that created the Joe Hill legend.

Yet in both history and law, perceptions of the participants are real, and we must account for them. It is perceived that Joe Hill was prosecuted for labor activities. To understand why the legal system was not sympathetic to Hill and his supporters, we must look into the process of judicial thought.

II

Experience not Logic

In 1880, future Supreme Court Justice Oliver Wendell Holmes gave a series of lectures at the Lowell Institute in Boston. Holmes' subject was the Anglo-American Common Law. For generations, judges had decided cases on the basis of cases that had come before. The lawyers and judges of the time believed they were making logical decisions based upon firmly settled points of law. Holmes set this notion on its ear. He spoke from a written text that was published as *The History of the Common Law* in 1881.

> The object of this book is to present a general view of the Common Law. To accomplish the task, other tools are needed besides logic. It is to something to show that the consistency of a system requires a particular result, but it is not all. The life of the law has not been logic: it has been experience. The felt necessities of the time, the prevalent moral and political theories, intuitions of public policy, avowed or unconscious, even the prejudices which Judges share with their fellow-men have had a good deal more to do than the syllogism in determining the rules by which men should be governed.

It is generally thought that Holmes was looking to the future in which judicial decisions were made in response to changing political and social circumstances.[31] Holmes was also indicting the jurisprudence of his day. The judges thought they were applying inflexible rules of logic when they were only enforcing the beliefs and norms of a ruling class. According to Holmes, they were more beholden to their upper class status than they were to pure logic.

It is impossible to exaggerate the formal legalism that dominated the courts in the era of industrialization. The generation was dominated by the case of *Lochner v. People of New York.*[32] The New York legislature passed a law limiting the hours of bakery workers to sixty per week. Joseph Lochner, owner of a Utica bakery, committed an offense and paid a fine. He became stubborn after being charged with a second offense, refused to pay, and was convicted. He appealed to the New York courts, and the conviction was affirmed. He was still not willing to pay a minor fine and appealed to the United States Supreme Court.

Justice Peckham wrote the Court's opinion. The Court found that the New York legislation limiting working hours violated the Fourteenth Amendment "as an arbitrary interference with personal liberty and private property, without due process of law." The Court distinguished a prior case, *Holden v. Hardy.*[33] In *Holden*, the Court had approved a Utah statute limiting work hours in mines and mills. The difference, according to the Court, was that mine labor was dangerous and limiting the hours was an attempt to improve safety and thus proper under the state's police power. According to Justice Peckham, no one ever claimed that working in a bakery was dangerous.

Not surprisingly, Justice Holmes dissented.

> This case is decided upon an economic theory which a large part of the country does not entertain . . . It is settled by various decisions of this court that state constitutions and state laws may regulate life in many ways which we as legislators might think injudicious, or if you like tyrannical, as this, and which equally interfere with the liberty to contract ... The 14th Amendment does not enact Mr. Herbert Spencer's Social Statistics[34] ... Some of these laws embody convictions or prejudices which judges are likely to share. Some may not. But a Constitution is not intended to embody a particular economic theory, whether of paternalism and the organic relation of the citizen to the state or of *laissez faire*. It is made for people of fundamentally differing views ...

> General propositions do not decide concrete cases; every opinion tends to become a law. I think the word "liberty" in

the 14th Amendment, is perverted when it is held to prevent the natural outcome of a dominant opinion unless it can be said that a rational and fair man would admit that the statute proposed would infringe fundamental principles as they have been understood by the traditions of our people and our law.

Lochner caused continued difficulties with union organizing. One of the problems unions faced was the "yellow-dog contract." This was a contract whereby the worker promised not to join a union. In 1898, congress passed a law precluding such contracts in the railroad business. Traditionally, congress was viewed as having such powers under the Inter-State Commerce Clause of the constitution. However, in a 1908 case, *Adair v. United States*,[35] the Court followed *Lochner* and found the law unconstitutional under the freedom to contract provisions of the Fourteenth Amendment. It was therefore legally within the rights of the employer to fire a union member.

Predictably, Holmes dissented. He found that hiring union members was a very limited infringement on the freedom of contract. "The section simply prohibits the more powerful party to exact certain undertakings, or to threaten dismissal or unjustly discriminate on certain grounds against those already employed ... I confess that I think that the right to make contracts at will that has been derived from the work [word] liberty in the Amendments has been stretched to its extreme by the decisions ..."

Adair was followed by *Coppage v. Kansas*[36] where the Court struck a state law precluding "yellow-dog" contracts on the same due process freedom to contract grounds. Homes again dissented. "In present conditions a workman not unnaturally may believe that only by belonging to a union can he secure a contract that will be fair to him. In that belief, whether right or wrong, may be held by a reasonable man, it seems to me that it may be enforced by law in order to establish the equality of position between the parties in which liberty of contract begins."

Lochner was not overruled until Franklin Roosevelt threatened to "pack the Court" with more progressive justices. It was extreme legal formulism to find rights for the employer in the Fourteenth Amendment. Logic and legalism led the Court to conclude that the employer's freedom of contract precluded legislation designed to protect the worker's freedom from extreme conditions and his right to organize and collectively bargain. Holmes was right in his observation that the decisions were not based upon logic but upon the prevailing notions of public policy held by the Court. Holmes protested not only against the use of "logic" but also the adoption of regressive social theory.[37]

III

Exploitation of the Courts

Holmes's observation that the courts of his time decided matters on the perceived needs of the day was best illustrated by the sad case of the Chicago Haymarket defendants. In 1886, after more than a decade of increasingly violent labor protests, a meeting was held at Haymarket Square. The police mobilized a large force, which moved in to break up the meeting. Someone (and that someone was never identified) threw a dynamite bomb into the police ranks. This led to a general outbreak of violence, with casualties on both sides.

Unable to indict the bomb thrower, the authorities charged the labor organizers. Ultimately, eight were convicted, with seven sentenced to death. This was the first great labor trial. Mass movements organized against the execution. Two sentences were commuted to terms in prison. The governor supposedly suggested that he would have commuted the other sentences had the labor leaders requested his action. Ultimately, four were hung, and one committed suicide before execution. Governor Altgeld pardoned the remaining leaders in 1890.

There are some things that may be said for certain about this sad matter. The most important is that the leaders were unquestionably innocent of throwing the bomb. The second is that the case is an example of the bitter contest between labor leaders and the establishment. Reading the opinion of the Illinois Supreme Court[38] at a distance of 120 years, one is struck by the desperation of the laboring class and the determination of the upper class to snuff out any notion of equality. The court's opinion cites for page after dreary page statements of various labor leaders. It must be admitted that the labor movement was largely composed of anarchists, but it must equally be admitted that the leaders had tried and failed to win concessions within the confines of elections and strikes.

The trial and execution of the Haymarket martyrs is an example of Justice Holmes's observation that the court system responds to the perceived needs of the day. The civic leaders in Chicago well understood that they were using the court system to intimidate and control labor. John Graham Brooks quotes a lawyer in the Ettor and Giovannitti case. The IWW had led a strike in Massachusetts, and the leaders of the union were charged but acquitted of the murder of a bystander. "But severity might have worked best, as it did in hanging the Chicago anarchists in '87. There was little enough justice there, but the thing worked. You haven't heard of anarchists in that town since."[39]

For forty years after Haymarket, labor fought its battles in the courtroom. For the most part, the charges were brought against union leaders. These charges were not based upon what the leaders had done but what they said. The legal theory was "conspiracy." Traditionally, in English and American law, the prosecutor needed to show agreement among the conspirators as well as an overt act toward accomplishing the crime. As time went by, the overt act became less and less a formality. Sen. William Borah of Idaho, as special prosecutor in the death of former Governor Frank Steunenberg, stated the proposition:

> It has been said that Mr. Haywood is not guilty notwithstanding Simpkins or Pettibone or Orchard or the others may be. But I want to call your attention a moment to the law under which the defendant is being tried. But I want to say before going to the law of conspiracy, in fairness to the defendant, that he cannot be made unwittingly a member of conspiracy. I concede that to start with. He cannot be made a member of a combination without his knowledge and willful design and purpose to join it. In other words if Pettibone and Orchard combined to commit this crime and did commit it under the feet of Mr. Haywood, without his knowingly and willfully joining the conspiracy, he is entitled to his acquittal.

But if we have proven a conspiracy in this case ... if the evidence in this case shows they were acting in concert, led on by the same purpose, one doing one thing and another one, one helping here and another there, then the act of one becomes the act of all ... After the agreement is in existence and they have become willfully and knowingly members thereof understanding the crime is to be committed or about to be committed, that from that time on they are one, they are partners, the act of one binds all.[40]

Down through the decades, the employers found one conspiracy after another. "General" Buckley Wells, the representative of the mine owners in Telluride, Colorado, tried his best time after time to find an excuse to hang Vincent St. John. The Haywood trial itself was a prominent allegation of conspiracy by the leaders of the Western Federation of Miners to murder Governor Stuenenberg. The Ettor case involved allegation of conspiracy by the IWW. A labor leader named Tom Mooney was alleged to have conspired to commit murder in a 1916 preparedness day parade in San Francisco. The authorities indicted the McNamara brothers for the bombing of the Los Angeles Times building. These are only the most prominent examples; there were conspiracies throughout the country. Even in the Sacco and Vanzetti trial, there is strong evidence that their indictment was based as much upon their anarchism as their actions.

It is clear that the conspiracy charges had little to do with guilt or innocence. Vincent St. John neither committed nor conspired to commit a violent act at any time in his life. The Haymarket martyrs were guilty of nothing more than language. Ettor and Giovanitti were guilty of nothing. Tom Mooney was beyond doubt innocent. On the other hand, the McNamara brothers were unquestionably guilty. At this juncture in time, anyone who ventures an opinion on the guilt or innocence of Sacco and Vanzetti should seriously question his sound judgment. As we will see, the same is true of Joe Hill.

IV
Trial Lawyers in the Labor Cases

The one factor in all of these trials that remains unexamined is the quality of trial counsel. Trial lawyers are not fungible. When writing about the great labor trials, authors seem to believe that the lawyers had little or nothing to do with the outcome. It is as if a jury will inevitably come to a conclusion of innocence regardless of the trial presentation.

Clarence Darrow succeeded in the Boise Haywood trial because he was a great lawyer and gave one of the greatest closing arguments of all time. (And perhaps he succeeded because he tainted the jury with bribes.) Judge Orin Hilton, Joe Hill's last lawyer, succeeded brilliantly in a long string of labor trials. On the other hand, in the great 1919 IWW trial in Chicago, George Vanderveer was often drunk and incomprehensible. In between these extremes was the Haymarket case, where not even Darrow could have stopped the legal lynching.

Part of the reason labor does not consider the quality of the lawyers is because the lawyers themselves did not always appreciate the propaganda value of their cases. Even Clarence Darrow failed to understand the propaganda defeat when he pled the McNamara brothers guilty in the *Los Angeles Times* bombing case.

Judge Hilton also disregarded the propaganda value of labor trials. At the request of Elizabeth Gurley Flynn, Judge Hilton represented some immigrant IWW workers charged with murder in Minnesota. Judge Hilton concluded that the defendants were in fact guilty and negotiated a favorable plea. This case led to Gurley Flynn and Ettor leaving the IWW as Bill Haywood considered pleading a worker guilty a lost opportunity for propaganda. Hilton never handled another labor case.

The trial skills of Fred Moore in the Sacco and Vanzetti trial are so lacking as to make any judgment about the proper outcome of that case impossible. A reading of the Sacco case leads to firm conclusions. The murder of a shoe company paymaster and his guard occurred in broad daylight in front of hundreds of witnesses. The entire incident took only seconds or at most minutes. It takes less than a trial genius to conclude that the eyewitness testimony was worthless because the witnesses' testimony was more impression than observation. Such witness testimony could have been easily impeached.

The evidence against the defendants consisted primarily of two categories. The defendants told gross fabrications about their activities when arrested. (They told these lies primarily because they were anarchists and may have been involved in a bombing campaign.) The major controversy was over physical evidence, most particularly ballistics. The defendants were armed to the teeth when arrested. Sacco had three types of ammunition on his person. The prosecution argued that one of the bullets fired into the paymaster was from Sacco's gun and of the same type of ammunition. Incredibly, no one on behalf of the defendants secured the physical evidence. There was not a problem in the chain of custody; there was no chain of custody. Instead of firming up the ballistics case, Moore chased every conspiracy rumor in the land.[41]

The obvious defense was reasonable doubt. Yet Moore persisted in putting the defendants on the witness stand in spite of the fact that they were easily impeachable by the false stories they had told the authorities. Propaganda was more important than a proper legal defense. Moore and the defendants wished to testify as to the merits of anarchism. There was no sound reason to expose the defendants to cross examination, particularly when they had demonstrated the ability to lie at will.

Even stranger was the way Moore conducted the presentation of witnesses. Moore called about one hundred witnesses, some for not more than five minutes. There was neither rhyme nor reason to the order and import of their testimony. Rather than tell a coherent and convincing story, Moore simply confused the jury and historians thereafter.

Moore's conduct should not have been a surprise to anyone knowing his history. There is only one recorded appellate case handled by Moore. A year before Sacco, Moore represented a murder defendant in California. The appellate court found no reason for his actions. Moore voluntarily introduced evidence that the defendant was an undesirable alien, in the process of being deported, and an active member of the IWW. On appeal, Moore argued that his actions as trial counsel prejudiced his client before the jury. The California court found this argument disingenuous. The only explanation for these strange trial and appellate tactics was Moore's primary loyalty to the labor movement and not the defendant.[42]

Moore had been involved on the edges of numerous labor cases but had little experience as a "first chair" trial lawyer. Assisting in the 1919 Chicago case, he became depressed and disappeared for weeks. Bill Haywood lost confidence in him when he characteristically failed to timely file a notice of appeal. After being relieved of his duties in Sacco, Moore returned to the west coast, where his mental health suffered. At the end of his life, he was insisting that his clients were in fact guilty. The simple fact is that Fred Moore was never physically or psychologically capable of handling the responsibilities of a major case. He was not capable of telling a convincing story.

The reason Moore was even on the case had nothing to do with his skill as a lawyer. Moore was a friend of Elizabeth Gurley Flynn and had a consistent and reliable ideological background. His legal judgment was flawed, but his propaganda value was high. It that sense, he did not disappoint.

V
A Dangerous Game

Representing labor defendants in the age of industrialization was a most dangerous game. The lawyers were literally playing with their clients' lives. Successful defense could be done and was done but often at the cost of disappointing the labor movement. It is not surprising that the most successful lawyers, Darrow and Hilton, exercised independent judgment. Darrow was the philosopher king with spellbinding skills to go with his skepticism. Hilton was a master of evidence and courtroom procedure. He was prepared and able to pounce upon any weakness showed by the prosecution. Yet, both were ultimately found wanting on ideological grounds by labor movement. Loyalty to the defendant was not enough. The labor lawyers were expected to win and win spectacularly. They were expected to deliver the message of the movement, along with the deliverance of the defendant.

The law was against the lawyers. The judges were constrained by their formal legalism. The jury pools were prejudiced against the defendants. Yet, skill could win, and lack of skill could guarantee disaster.

As we will see in the trial court of Joe Hill's case, ideology and propaganda were pursued at the cost of sound legal advice. The trial lawyers, MacDougal and Scott, were local socialists who took the opportunity to explain socialism, perhaps at the cost of Hill's life. They were also seeking local notoriety. Perhaps no one could have won Hill's case, but he would certainly have had a better chance with Darrow or Hilton presenting the defense.

Chapter 4

A Hard Place to Try a Case

The chief end of man is to frame general ideas and no general idea is worth a damn.

Justice Oliver Wendell Holmes

I

A Salt Lake City Jury

Any lawyer worth his salt is concerned about the location of his trial. He has to concern himself with both the judges and the jury pool. In modern times, millions of dollars are spent on jury research and community image preparation. When faced with his financial fraud case, the billionaire Michael Milken hired a public relations firm to study the dynamics of a New York jury and how to appeal to their prejudices. He went so far as to provide hundreds of New York Yankee tickets so that he could be seen at the game with underprivileged children. (It did not work. He had to plead guilty, and Judge Kimba Woods was not impressed with his charity.)

The good labor lawyers paid much attention to the jury pool. It is reported that in the Bill Haywood case, Clarence Darrow surveyed every potential jury member in Canyon County. When the trial was moved to Ada County, his team repeated the feat. Given Darrow's indictment for jury tampering in California, one might suspect that his attention to jury detail may have crossed the line into improper attempts to reach the jury pool.

Joe Hill's last lawyer, Judge Orin Hilton, was also a master of jury relations. In the Colorado murder trial of Steve Adams, a labor suspect, Hilton knew he would get no miners on the jury. The prosecution's theory of the case was that a mine manager was assassinated by a shotgun. The prosecution witnesses were to testify that the shot was fired from distance. Instead of miners, Hilton filled the jury box with ranchers and farmers, to whom shotguns were a necessary tool. They knew how pellets scattered, and they quickly discerned the impossibility of the prosecution strategy.

In defending Joe Hill, the lawyers needed to know the community in which he was charged. Utah in 1914 was a difficult place to perceive community attitudes and shape Hill's defense in a manner that would appeal to local prejudice. Salt Lake County might have been the headquarters of the Mormon Church, but it was also the commercial hub of non-Mormon Utah. Further, it was the location of Bingham Canyon, the largest copper mine in the world, with thousands of immigrant non-Mormon miners.

The Joe Hill matter would be fought out against this disparate background. Throughout the last century, the simple labor explanation was that a Mormon jury was reactionary in convicting Joe Hill. The truth is much more complicated. The Joe Hill jury would include traditional Mormons but also non-Mormon laborers. It also included a baptized Mormon who went to Seattle and worked on the docks—a traditional IWW labor stronghold.

Therefore, we must attempt to understand the makeup of the Salt Lake County jury pool and the attitudes of the Utah Judiciary.

II

Mormons and Corporations

In 1911, Frank J. Cannon wrote a book entitled *Under the Prophet in Utah*. Cannon was a controversial figure in Utah. He was the son of

Mormon apostle and member of the Church's First Presidency, George Q. Cannon. Although personally loyal to his family, Frank had always stood somewhat aloof from the membership of the Church. He was the territorial representative to congress and played some part in the negotiations that led to statehood. At statehood there was a community agreement that the new state's senate seats would be filled by a Mormon and a non-Mormon. The first state legislature chose Frank Cannon to fill the Mormon seat.

Cannon was always somewhat of a political renegade. Elected as a Republican, he soon deserted the party on the issue of silver coinage. He served but one term in the senate, being soundly defeated for reelection by the legislature. Cannon then went on to become chairman of the Utah Democratic party.

After leaving the senate, Cannon, with his outstanding journalistic skills, became editor of the *Salt Lake Tribune* and later the *Ogden Standard*. Both papers were openly antagonistic to the Mormon Church and in particular the then-current Church president Joseph F. Smith. Smith was the nephew of founding church president, Joseph Smith. In the senate challenge to apostle Reed Smoot assuming his seat, Cannon, along with the protestant establishment, saw Smith as backtracking on the Mormon commitment to abolish polygamy. Cannon's opposition to Smith degenerated into vitriol. Cannon spent the remaining years of his life writing and speaking in opposition to Mormonism. Indeed, much of his book was nothing more than the standard anti-Mormonism of the day.

The Mormons traditionally regard Frank Cannon as an ingrate apostate. Whatever Cannon was before and whatever he later became, in 1911 he was a frustrated progressive. Cannon's book looks back to the heroic age of Mormon settlement in the intermountain west. He lauds the community efforts needed to settle the Great Basin. The people worked together on irrigation and building community resources. Cannon recalled the earlier revelations establishing communal enterprise as opposed to individual aggrandizement. In the early Utah period, faithful Mormons paid tithing to the local bishop "in kind." The bishop would be the custodian of eggs, wheat, sheep, or whatever else the community produced. The early bishops had great authority in distributing those products to the needs of the community. To Cannon, this system was transparent. The people could see the benefit of their sacrifice.

Cannon's chief complaint was that after the establishment of a cash economy, tithing was paid in dollars and cents. The money went to the general church and was controlled by President Smith. Cannon saw this accumulation of money as dangerous to the institutions of the state. There is some basis to Cannon's complaint about the lack of transparency. Monies were expended by the "Council on the Disposition of Tithes" under the direction of President Smith. Cannon linked the centralization of fund collection with the great trusts and industrial organizations of the country. He felt that this centralization of Church funds should be curtailed like the Northern Railroad and Standard Oil.

> To him (Joseph F. Smith) the Mormon people pay a yearly tribute of more than two million dollars in tithes; and he uses that income to his own ends, without an accounting. He is president of the Utah branch of the sugar trust and of the local incorporation of the salt trust; and he supports the exaction's of monopoly by his financial absolutism, while he defends them from competition by his religious power ... He is president of a system of "company stores," from which the faithful buy their merchandise; of a wagon and machine company from which the Mormon farmers purchase their vehicles; of life-insurance and fire insurance companies, of banking institutions, of a knitting company of newspapers ... and ruling the non-Mormons of Utah, as he rules his own people, by virtue of his political and financial partnership with the great "business interests" that govern and exploit this nation, and his kingdom, for their own gain and his.

Frank Cannon was not the only person to link the interests of the Mormon Church to "business interests." Leonard Arrington, in the seminal Mormon history *Great Basin Kingdom,* notes:

> Coincident with the Smoot investigation a "crusade" was launched in a number of national magazines designed to "expose" and destroy the "tyranny" of the church,

particularly in the field of business. In such magazines as *McClure's, Everybody's, Pearson's* and *Cosmopolitan*—and even in such august journals as the *North American Review* and the *Atlantic*—the church was referred to as a viper and a lawbreaker, and it's business interests were linked up with the current bugaboo, "the trusts."[43]

Indeed, according to British newspapers, the Church was believed to "draw a hundred percent dividend from the Rubber Trust; to have an interest in the National City Bank and to have controlling interests in the wool, beef, tin, oil, tobacco, iron and farming implement industries."

Of course, these reported connections to the great industrial combinations of the progressive era are fanciful. A poor agrarian people in the Great Basin were hardily competition for Carnegie and Rockefeller. When Frank Cannon got specific, he could only point to the Church's investment in sugar beets and salt distillation at the Great Salt Lake.

Whether true or not, there was great perception of the alignment of the Mormon Church with the industrial concerns of the day. These perceptions spilled over into the Utah law courts.

In 1908, the Utah Supreme Court heard an appeal designated as *Paul v. Salt Lake City R. Co.*[44] Louisa P. Paul sued the Salt Lake street car company. The company was organized by the Church. Church President Joseph F. Smith was also president of the company. The cause of action was for negligence. Mrs. Paul was injured while leaving one of the company's street cars.

In 1908, Utah, like every other state, followed the doctrine of "contributory negligence." This was a severe doctrine, holding that if the injured party was in some way negligent in her conduct, she could not recover damages even if the majority of fault lay with the defendant. Through statute and case law, every jurisdiction now rejects this doctrine and provides recovery on the basis of a comparison of negligence between the parties.

In this trial, the jury found that Mrs. Paul contributed to her own injuries. The majority of the opinion (written by Justice Frick with Chief Justice

Straup in concurrence) is not particularly remarkable in the jurisprudence of the day. The opinion approves jury instructions indicating that the occurrence of an accident is not evidence of negligence. The court indicates that there is no presumption of negligence from the injury of Mrs. Paul on the company's premises.

However, the case is unusual. Mrs. Paul's lawyer, S. P. Armstrong,[45] filed a post-judgment motion for a new trial. The basis of this motion was an affidavit, signed by Armstrong. The affidavit stated that subsequent to the verdict, Mr. Armstrong learned of "interference by the president of the respondent which tended to pervert the course of justice and prevented plaintiff (Mrs. Paul) from having a fair trial." Specifically the affidavit provided:

> That Joseph F. Smith was, at all times stated in the affidavit, the president of respondent (the street car company) and also the president, prophet, seer and revelator of the Church of Jesus Christ of Latter-day Saints, a religious organization with a large membership in Salt Lake City and county. Affiant (Mr. Armstrong), on information and belief states that one of the cardinal doctrines of said church is obedience to the teachings, utterances, and instructions of its prophet, seer and revelator; that affiant is informed and believes that the said Joseph F. Smith, the president of said church and of respondent, at a secret priesthood meeting held at the Tabernacle in Salt Lake City on the evening of April 7, 1906, took occasion to instruct his religious followers as to their duties if called upon to serve as jurors in the trial of cases against corporations, and particularly street railway corporations, and that he stated, in substance, "that there were grafters in the country seeking by every possible trick to secure verdicts against corporations by means of damage suits; that people will step off street cars and pretend to suffer injuries which did not exist and lawyers would take such personal injury cases and by such trickery secure verdicts against corporations.

Further, Mr. Armstrong stated that Joseph F. Smith regretted that Latter-day Saints, sitting as jurors, returned verdicts against corporations. Armstrong represented that the intent of Smith's words was to induce the Latter-day Saints to look with great suspicion on suits against corporations. Mr. Armstrong alleged that five of the jurors were Latter-day Saints and that one of them was an official in the Church.

Justice Frick found that not a single fact in the affidavit was stated with personal knowledge. Mr. Armstrong did not claim that any of the jurors were present at the supposed meeting. None of them heard the alleged statements. The affidavit was insufficient to support the claim for a new trial, as there was no personal knowledge of actual jury tampering. "Is it to be presumed that simply because a juror is a member of a certain religious organization and believes in its doctrines and tenets, therefore a court can assume that he hears and knows of all matters that may be said by any official of the organization upon any and all subjects and further assume that he would follow and be controlled by what such official may have said of which the juror is supposed to be informed constructively?"

Mr. Armstrong made a clear challenge to the seating of Mormon jurors "based upon the theory that the expressed wish or desire of the president of the church, upon all subjects, will be implicitly followed by all of the members of the church." The implication of Armstrong's challenge was clear. Keep all Mormons off of jury duty, particularly in cases involving corporations. In rejecting Armstrong's argument, the Utah Supreme Court refused to disenfranchise the members of the Church.

Further, Justice Frick defended the constitutional rights of church members to believe or teach what they desired concerning corporations and jury service. He said that "Mr. Smith" had every right to freely communicate with the members of his church so long as there was no attempt to directly communicate with the jurors. It was implied that jury verdicts would not be overturned by allegations of church influence, even regarding corporations.

The Utah Supreme Court did show deferential treatment of the Church and its leaders in the early twentieth century. A 1910 case, *Grant v. Lawrence,*[46] demonstrates exactly how far the court would go to avoid distress to prominent church leaders. Heber J. Grant was a member of the Church's twelve apostles. (Grant succeeded Joseph F. Smith as church president.) Like all apostles of the day, excepting Reed Smoot, Grant was polygamous. In 1910, he was married to two women.

Grant opened the church mission in Japan. He spent two years in the country. He took one of his wives, Augusta, to the Orient. Upon returning to Salt Lake City, he built a substantial home on South Temple Street for Augusta. Grant was then called to preside over the Church's European missions. When he left for London, Augusta remained home in Salt Lake City. In her place, Grant took his other wife, Emily.

While still in London, Grant was sued by Franklin Lawrence. To start a suit, the defending party must be served. Service is usually made personally on the defendant by handing him a copy of the complaining papers. Lawrence could not personally serve Grant as Grant was not in the country. Lawrence then attempted "substitute service," a procedure allowed by every American jurisdiction. This service is made by delivering the papers to a person of suitable age at the residence of the defendant. Lawrence served Augusta at the South Temple house.

Upon returning to Utah, Grant brought suit to set aside the judgment Lawrence had obtained on the basis that he had not been properly served. Grant argued that his usual place of abode was not with his polygamous wife, Augusta, as he was living in England with Emily.

Justice Frick agreed with Grant's argument. Even though continued polygamy was an open secret in Utah, the court would not presume that service on a polygamous wife was sufficient.

The *Grant* case is not the only example of the court showing deference to the church and its leaders. All of the pre-1914 Utah Supreme Court decisions involving the church or its leaders find in favor of the church. These would include ordinary business cases and arbitration cases. For the better part of two decades, a primary concern of the court was untangling the probate affairs of polygamous men. The court showed surprising deference to the Church doctrine of "Celestial Marriage."

II

Utah and Politics

Utah in the second decade of the twentieth century was a very conservative jurisdiction. The easiest demonstration is the four-way presidential race of 1912. Theodore Roosevelt (to whom the Mormons owed a great debt through resolution of the Reed Smoot senatorial contest) came home from a tour of Africa and Europe to discover that his hand-picked successor, William Howard Taft, had departed from progressive principles. Taft demonstrated that in fact he was rather conservative. Roosevelt challenged Taft for the Republican nomination. Roosevelt won most of the popular primaries, but Taft, controlling the party mechanism, obtained the nomination. Roosevelt, believing himself cheated out of the nomination, formed the Progressive Party. At his competing convention, Roosevelt proclaimed that the country "Stood at Armageddon." His party, commonly denominated as the "Bull Moose" party, stood for progressive ideals, such as women's suffrage, direct election of senators, and restraints on corporations and business trusts.

After a number of ballots, the Democrats nominated their own progressive, Woodrow Wilson. The Socialist Party, then at the pinnacle of its power, nominated their perennial candidate, Eugene Debs. Debs would have been the most radical candidate, with Roosevelt second and Wilson third. Taft was clearly the most conservative man in the race.

Nationally, the vote was split. The solid South voted for Wilson, a native of Virginia. The national progressive vote was split between Roosevelt and Wilson. The Republican vote was split between Taft and Roosevelt. Under those conditions, Wilson prevailed. In the popular and electoral vote, Roosevelt was second. Taft was a distant third.

Taft won the electoral votes of only Vermont and Utah. In Utah, Taft carried every county with the exception of the labor-dominated Carbon County, which voted for Debs. It was a stunning demonstration of statewide conservatism. It is further telling to note that Theodore Roosevelt was not second in Utah votes but trailed Woodrow Wilson.

Further confirmation of Utah's conservatism is found in the senators serving from the state. At that time, senators were still elected by the state legislature. The Mormon senator, apostle Reed Smoot survived the challenge to his seat by evangelical Christianity, only to become a conservative or even reactionary member of the senate. It is amusing to note that Senator Smoot was too radical for the religious tastes of the day but became the fervent defender of the status quo. He believed in preserving American business interests through protectionism. His career was capped by the Smoot-Hawley Tariff Bill, widely acknowledged as a prime contributor to the depth of the Great Depression.

The non-Mormon senator, George Sutherland, was appointed to the Supreme Court by President Harding. There he set a record for conservative jurisprudence that has never been seriously challenged. During the Great Depression, Sutherland was one of Franklin Roosevelt's "nine old men" sitting on the Supreme Court. Sutherland, with his fellow conservatives, struck down much of the New Deal legislation as violations of the constitution's Commerce Clause. It was Sutherland, in particular, who provoked Roosevelt's court-packing project. It was only with the retirement of Sutherland and his fellow conservatives that New Deal legislations became law.

Because the senators were elected by the legislature, the people through their representatives demonstrated consistent conservative voting habits. The first three governors of the state were Mormons. The first governor, Daniel Wells, was the son of a close associate of Brigham Young. The governor in 1914 was William Spry, who rose to prominence as the president of the Latter-day Saint Southern Mission.

In considering Mormon and Utah conservatism, it would be a mistake to blindly add nativism. In 1914, Mormons had established missions in foreign countries for more than seventy-five years. A large percentage of the Mormon people were foreign born. General authorities Talmage and Roberts were born in Great Britain. There was a large group of Scandinavian converts scattered about the state. Mormonism's second scholar apostle, John A. Widsoe, was Norwegian.

In fact, multinational Utah births are clearly demonstrated by the men who served on the Joe Hill jury. Six of the twelve who served were not native born. Juror number four, Rudolph Boss, was born in Switzerland. Juror number five, John Alvin Hillstead, juror number seven, John Garbett, and juror number eleven, Fred A. Robinson, were born in England.[47] Juror number eight, Thomas Joseph Owen, was born in Wales. Juror number nine, Robert McDowell, was born in Ireland. Even among the foreign born, Utah was a conservative jurisdiction. Hill's lawyer, Ernest MacDougall's, closing argument attacked the fairness of the Utah establishment. It was a speech that a socialist such as MacDougall might have made anywhere in the country. It did not resonate in conservative Utah.

III

The Mormons and the Miners

If there was a population division in Utah other than religion, it was one of class and ethnicity. Starting about 1890, coal and hard-rock mining began in Utah. With the exception of "Uncle" Jesse Knight, the owners of these mines were rich non-Mormons. For example, the Carbon County coal mines were owned by the Utah Fuel Company, a division of the Rio Grande Railroad. The massive open pit copper mine at Bingham Canyon was financed and owned by the Guggenheim family.

To operate these mines, foreign workers from Italy, Greece, and the Austria-Hungarian Empire were imported. These workers were non-Mormon and existed in what seems to be a parallel universe. Mormons had little to do with them, and they had little to do with Mormons.

The vast majority of these workers were unskilled labor. They were paid little, worked long and dangerous hours, and lived in harsh circumstances. There were two major work stoppages in Utah. One was roughly contemporaneous with the foundation of the Industrial Workers of the World. This occurred in the Carbon County Coal mines. The other was at the Bingham Canyon Copper mine. This strike was directed by the Western Federation of Miners, although the IWW would later take credit.

The important distinction in both strikes was that the laborers were southern Europeans and non-Mormons. Indeed, the Mormons were scarcely interested. It is only through the reaction of the authorities, particularly the Mormon governors Daniel Wells and William Spry, that we discern Mormon thought on these foreign labor interlopers in their Great Basin Kingdom.

The story of the 1903–1904 Carbon County coal strike has been documented by Dr. Alan Kent Powell.[48] He tells of the efforts of the United Mine Workers to organize a labor force that was mostly Italian. As the strike became more general, Governor Heber Wells detailed the head of the Utah National Guard, General John Q. Cannon (Frank Cannon's brother), to investigate the situation. On General Cannon's advice, Governor Wells dispatched a portion of the National Guard to the scene. These guardsmen were from the Sanpete Valley and would have been Latter-day Saints.

The National Guard was instructed to protect company property and assist local law enforcement. One of their tasks was to assist the sheriff in arresting the chief union organizer. Dr. Powell records that by the time their service was ended, many of the soldiers felt sympathy for the strikers.

The chief LDS influence in the strike came from Angus M. Cannon (Frank Cannon's uncle). Angus Cannon was president of the Salt Lake Stake, which at that time covered the entire valley. Angus Cannon announced that employment was available for anyone who wanted it in Carbon County. The inducement to Mormon strikebreakers was short lived. The Church's First Presidency, over the signature of Joseph F. Smith, announced neutrality in the labor dispute.[49]

The strike ultimately failed, and the Italian workers were replaced by another non-Mormon group of miners from Greece.

The 1912 Bingham Canyon strike barely touched the lives of the Latter-day Saints. The best source on this strike is an article by Gunther Peck.[50] Bingham Canyon had been worked for years as individual mines. By 1905, the Utah Copper Company had been formed by Daniel Jackling. Jackling's vision was to mine the low-grade copper ore found in abundance. This required the use of steam power in railroads and mining machinery. The old-time miners who worked underground were replaced by the unskilled labor needed to empty railroad cars and constantly move railroad tracks. The workers were Italian, Greek, and Japanese. Skilled labor tended to be Swedish. Mormons were hardly visible. Dr. Peck states that the Bingham Canyon Branch of the Church attracted between twenty-five and fifty members to weekly services.

The significant Mormon involvement was the proposed intervention by Governor William Spry. Both miners and owners solicited the services of Spry, who demonstrated a lack of fundamental knowledge about industrial mining. The Guggenheims owned other copper mines and merely increased their production at other locations. Further, a new group of non-Mormons, Mexican immigrants, were brought into the mine as strike breakers. The strike broke up with mutual recrimination among the ethnic groups.

This is not to imply that Latter-day Saints were completely divorced from the mining industry. Frank Cannon thought President Joseph F. Smith was entirely too close to the Utah Copper Company's Daniel Jackling. The brilliant Mormon president of the University of Utah and future apostle James E. Talmage was the foremost geologist of the era. He testified in numerous mining lawsuits as an expert witness. Indeed, he retired from the university to devote himself to the business of testimony. That retirement was short lived because of the call to the apostleship.

There was also "Uncle" Jesse Knight. Jesse Knight was the son of an important Latter-day Saint. His father, Newel Knight, was the leader of the first community to join the Mormon Church as a group. The Colesville Branch remained intact for many years. Newell Knight's visit to Joseph Smith was the occasion of the first recorded miracle in Mormon history.[51] Newel Knight served in many responsible positions, dying in 1850 on the plains while the Saints traveled to the Rocky Mountains.

Jesse Knight was born at Nauvoo, Illinois, on September 6, 1845. Left fatherless, he struggled for a living throughout his youth. He was, for a time, not consistent in his church activities. Uneducated, he had the rare gift of visualizing ore deposits from surface geology. In 1886, he discovered the fabulous Humbug Mine in the Tintic Mining District. Success followed success, and he acquired numerous other mines in the Eureka, Utah, area. Ultimately, he owned mines, farms, and sugar mills, all under the control of his Knight Investment Company.

Jesse Knight made money, but he also gave it away. Jesse and his wife, Amanda, saved the struggling Brigham Young University on numerous occasions. The location of the present campus was a gift from the Knight family. Knight also gave freely to the LDS Church.

Knight was also distinguished in his treatment of his employees. He founded the town of Knightville in Juab County. Rather than the usual hedonistic pleasures of mining camps, Knightville had a church and a recreation hall. When it was discovered that there were not enough children for a school, Knight hired a man with a large family. Knight was paternalistic, but his reputation for fair treatment of his workers was a far cry from that of the Utah Copper Company. Jesse Knight is an example of Mormonism in the mining camps who compares favorably to his fellows.[52] The case for Mormon exploitation of the emigrant mining community is therefore lacking. For the most part, the communities went their separate ways. But where they did cross, Mormon businessmen, such as Knight, were no worse and even better in their treatment of labor. With the exception of Angus Cannon, no Mormon leader interfered in the major labor difficulties.

It has long been presumed that the Joe Hill jury must have been composed of small businessmen or others constitutionally opposed to labor. This is not true. Mine workers were on the Joe Hill jury. John A. Hillstead was a mill man in the copper industry. Harry Thomas was the foreman of a powder plant. Other jury members were unskilled laborers. Ernest Alder was a teamster, but in the 1920 census, he had moved to Seattle, where he was a stevedore. John Garbett was a brakeman on a steam railway. Thomas Owen was a motorman on the street car railway. Again, there were jurors who might have been swayed with a proper deference to their sensibilities.

IV

Why the Mormons Were Conservative

It would be a mistake to view Utah as a conservative theocracy set in its ways for generations. It is true the Latter-day Saints were conservative. Their conservatism was born of a desperate need for acceptance by the nation in which they lived. It is not hard to find evidence of this insecurity. The brilliant young lawyer J. Reuben Clark was assistant solicitor of the state department. He lived in absolute fear that he would be dismissed on religious grounds. Writing in 1899, the equally brilliant James E. Talmage, president of the University of Utah and an apostle by the time of the Joe Hill trial, was defensive in defining the Saints' relationship to the nation.

> The Church of Jesus Christ of Latter-day Saints makes emphatic declaration of its belief and precepts regarding the duty of its members toward the laws of the land, and sustains its position by the authority of specific revelation in ancient as in present times. Moreover, the people are confident that when the true story of their rise and progress as an established body of religious worshipers is fully known, the loyalty of the Church and the patriotic devotion of its members will be vindicated and extolled by the world in general, as now by the few unprejudiced investigators who have studied with honest purpose the history of this remarkable organization.[53]

Apostle Reed Smoot was regularly elected to the senate in 1903. He was allowed to take his seat, but the senate thereafter began proceedings as to his qualifications after receiving a protest from the non-Mormon citizens of Utah. Interestingly, this protest was not only made by Protestant ministers from the various denominations but also by members of the business and mining communities.

The Smoot matter dragged on for the better part of three years. To the embarrassment of the church, it was revealed that some of the Church authorities had not been compliant with President Wilford Woodruff's 1890 manifesto on polygamy. Ultimately, two apostles, Mathias Cowley and John W. Taylor, resigned. President Joseph F. Smith suffered personal attacks, and to the minds of the country's non-Mormons, was greatly embarrassed in his testimony before the committee.[54]

After more than a century, the transcript of the Smoot hearing seems rather strange. In twenty-first-century America, citizens are familiar, if not comfortable with, Scientology, the Unification Church, and American Moslems. By the end of the hearing, polygamy had ceased to be the issue. The issue, as Kathleen Flake[55] demonstrates, was theology. In other words, "Did the First Amendment apply to all religion or only the Christian religions practiced by the majority?" In the later stages of the hearing, the non-Mormons' testimony centered on the Mormon temple ceremony. Mormons, of course, considered the temple rites to be sacred and certainly not something to be shared in a public hearing. The committee called a number of individuals who had left the Church to detail the various oaths and obligations undertaken by the faithful. Again, as Dr. Flake demonstrates, secret oaths and ceremonies were much more common to men in public life at the turn of the twentieth century than today. The Mormon temple ceremonies seemed much less threatening to senators who were Masons, Elks, Woodsmen, or Moose. In the end, on February 20, 1907, Senator Smoot was seated by a large majority of senators.

The Mormons understood the Smoot hearing to be a challenge to their theology. Following the Church's conference in April 1907, the Protestant ministers of Salt Lake City again published their old accusations against the Church. This time the Church replied publically. This address was given by B. H. Roberts, a Mormon intellectual, polygamist, and general authority of the Church, on June 17, 1907. Roberts's speech concerned itself for the most part with a defense of Mormon concepts of man and God. The Mormon God was real and tangible, as opposed to the traditional trinity. The Mormon God spoke to man. Mormons believed that mankind could progress to a higher status and even reach godhood themselves. Roberts ridiculed the Calvinism of the day, saying that it was barbaric in its notion of the election of the elite. In his speech, Roberts gave little attention to either the charge of polygamy or church domination.[56] The theological content of the political contests is most clearly demonstrated by the Idaho case of *Toneray v. Budge.*[57] The Idaho state constitution had a provision prohibiting voting by any member of a church teaching "Celestial Marriage." Toneray challenged the election of

Budge as a judge based upon his membership in the Mormon Church. The claim was that the Church still taught what Toneray termed "Celestial Marriage." The Idaho Court resorted to a number of Mormon-written teachings (particularly Dr. James E. Talmage's "Articles of Faith). Those church writings demonstrated the Mormon belief in the eternal nature of marriage and that although Mormons referred to their particular form of matrimony as "Celestial Marriage," the drafters of the constitution had used the term to refer to polygamy. As Budge, the elected official, had neither espoused nor practiced polygamy, his personal religious beliefs were irrelevant to his election. Thus, it was only in 1908 that the Mormon right to the franchise in Idaho was ultimately secured.

Even with Smoot's ultimate victory and the Idaho Court decision, Mormons were not politically secure in their own capital. In 1905, non-Mormons, led by ex-senators Frank Cannon and Thomas Kearns, organized the "American" Party. They were, for the most part, national Republicans. The American Party swept the Salt Lake Municipal Offices in 1905 and remained in power until 1911. The shock and dismay of the faithful is recounted by B. H. Roberts in his *Comprehensive History of the Church*.[58] Roberts records that it took a "strenuous effort" to overthrow the American party in the election of 1910.

V

Judicial Clay

The community is the clay from which the lawyer molds his case. Of course, the jury is picked from the members of the community. Judges also are unlikely to go beyond community norms in their decisions without compelling legal reasons. This was particularly true of the judges involved in Joe Hill's case. Judge Morris Ritchie was elected by the voters of Salt Lake County. The three justices of the Utah Supreme Court were elected statewide.

It is possible that the Joe Hill case could never have been won in Salt Lake City. Juries everywhere would have been suspicious of the alibi. Juries do not like cases that make no sense. To be successful, the lawyers would have had to play upon the Mormon insecurity about their status. Mormons had reason to suspect authority and had a long history of defying what they considered to be unjust oppression. The jury as selected had eight jurors identified with the LDS Church.[59] While the jury was unanimous in convicting Joe Hill, any one of the jurors, Mormon or non-Mormons, could have derailed the process.

Ernest D. MacDougall and Frank B. Scott, the trial attorneys, seemed oblivious to the Mormon population and philosophy of Salt Lake County. The appellate attorney, Judge Orin Hilton, openly mocked and vilified the Mormons. Neither approach was fruitful in defending Joe Hill.

Chapter 5

Two Wandering Socialist Lawyers

The main theme of the speech was socialism, its growth, and a prophecy of its ultimate success. With that we have nothing to do ...

Justice Oliver Wendell Holmes

I

Joe Hill's Lawyers

In 1965, a *New York Times* journalist, Anthony Lewis, wrote a book entitled *Gideon's Trumpet*. This was the story of Clarence Earl Gideon. Gideon was a petty criminal charged in the Florida courts with burglary. As he was impecunious, he respectfully requested the court appoint him a lawyer. At that time, Florida law only allowed for appointed counsel for indigents in cases involving the death penalty. The trial judge refused, so Gideon was convicted and filed a handwritten petition to the United States Supreme Court seeking a new trial on the grounds that he did not have a lawyer.

Petitions to the Supreme Court are rarely granted. They are closely screened by a staff of young lawyers for issues of national importance. The Court accepted Gideon's petition and appointed counsel to argue the case. Ultimately, the Court found that Gideon was correct; the Sixth Amendment right to counsel included a right to appointed counsel in the case of individuals who could not afford to hire lawyers.

Gideon v. Wainwright[60] has entered into national folklore. Hallmark Films produced a made for television movie. Henry Fonda played Gideon, Jose Ferrer played lawyer Abe Fortas, and John Houseman played Chief Justice Warren.

It is largely thought that Justice Black's opinion in *Gideon* was the first word on appointment of trial counsel. This is not true. The Supreme Court first considered appointing trial counsel in the 1932 case of the Scottsboro boys. In the early Depression years, young men of all races traveled the country in freight cars. Railroad detectives would attempt to catch them and put the off the train. In northern Alabama, just short of the Tennessee state line, railroad detectives caught nine black youths riding in a car with two white young women. According to the moirés of the day in the Deep South, such conduct was facial evidence of rape.

The young black men were given a speedy trial in a lynch mob atmosphere. All of the trials were finished within one day. Although local counsel was provided, the lawyer was operating under a death threat. He was assisted by a Tennessee real estate lawyer who admittedly knew nothing of Georgia criminal law or procedure. All white juries convicted the young men and sentenced them to death.

This injustice was too much for even a conservative Court. The reactionary Justice Sutherland (from Utah) wrote the opinion, which in reality had two facets.[61] First, in a death penalty case, the accused is entitled to counsel, and second, in a death penalty case, the Fourteenth Amendment guarantee of fairness and due process required effective assistance of counsel.

The Supreme Court reiterated its "flat" requirement of appointed counsel in a death penalty case in 1948.[62] Further, in 1954, the Court echoed the words of Justice Sutherland and held that a death penalty defendant was entitled to be heard through his own counsel at any stage of the proceeding.[63] "Even the intelligent and educated layman requires the guiding hand of counsel at every step in the proceedings against him."

This line of cases is important in considering the Joe Hill case because Joe Hill represented himself at arraignment and at the preliminary hearing. These violations would have been sufficient forty years later to overturn his conviction.

It is clear that the IWW would have provided counsel had Joe Hill asked the union for help. The union and its supporters raised money after the conviction that would have been sufficient to engage the best of counsel. It is hard to get inside of Joe Hill's head. At times he seems to think that he does not want the union spending money on him. At other times he seems to exude a childlike confidence in the fairness that the proceedings will deliver him without effort. He accepted help when help was volunteered after the jury convicted him, but he did not send for Ed Rowan, the local head of the IWW, until late in the process. Thus, at trial Joe Hill did not have the assistance of the excellent lawyers often retained by the labor movement.

We must note the lack of competence of the lawyers representing Joe Hill. Under the Rules of Professional Conduct, Rule 1.1[64] (which governs the conduct of lawyers in every jurisdiction except California), a lawyer can do something she has not done before. In Alaska, I handled many matters I had not done previously. I handled matters that no lawyer in Alaska had ever done before.[65] If a lawyer has not handled such a matter, she has to make herself competent by study and consulting with a lawyer who has been there before. There are often further requirements. In the modern state of Utah, if a criminal lawyer is going to handle a murder trial, she has to be "death penalty qualified." This means that she will have handled a number of criminal matters and assisted in a prior death penalty case.

Joe Hill's lawyers were not "Death Penalty" qualified. In actuality they had very little experience in trial advocacy. In the most important murder trial in the history of the state, Joe Hill was represented by Ernest D. MacDougall. The newspapers spell his name "McDougall," but he was rather consistent about having it "MacDougall."

This central character in the Joe Hill case is almost ignored by everyone with connection to the matter. Bill Haywood and Elizabeth Gurley Flynn did not know his name. The first time his name appeared in the Salt Lake

Press was at the opening of the Joe Hill trial, and then no description of him or his prior life experience was given.[66] Dr. Foner told us nothing about MacDougall and even misspelled his name.[67] Barrie Stavis did not even identify trial counsel. The same was true of Wallace Stegner. Even Gibbs Smith, who gave the most balanced treatment of the case, had no idea who MacDougall was or what his legal experience had been.[68]

The only physical description of MacDougall in the literature is by the cub reporter Rae Wellman. She described him as a striking contrast to Elmer Leatherwood, the prosecutor. "The district Attorney and the attorney for the defense afforded a striking contrast. He (Leatherwood) was large, heavy, with a harnessed face and a forceful deliberate manner of speech, conveying a slim conviction to one's mind of his somber sincerity: the other (MacDougall) a delicately coiled spring of a man, sputtering electrical sparks of fitting cross testimony in the occasional flashes of humor, more of impression than speech, that seemed to clear for a moment the prevailing heavy colorless atmosphere of the courtroom."[69]

It is difficult to locate MacDougall in history. There is no photograph of him. He was born in Ontario, Canada. We first find him in the 1900 Census. He was in Detroit at age twenty-one. He claimed to be a lawyer. This claim is only partially true. The Michigan Supreme Court shows a bar admission date of June 23, 1901. The Michigan bar has no further records, including records of schooling. The Michigan clerk of court felt that not unusual, as many if not most of the lawyers of the day were admitted after a legal clerkship and did not attend law school.

MacDougall's bar file at the Wyoming Supreme Court indicates that he was admitted to the practice of law in Michigan in 1900, which date is inaccurate, according to the Michigan records. Again, there is no record of school attendance. The Wyoming lawyer file also states that he was admitted in Colorado in 1901 and practiced between 1901 and 1902 in Cripple Creek, Colorado. The Colorado Supreme Court has no records of MacDougall being admitted to practice in that state. There is nothing about MacDougall in any of the secondary literature dealing with the significant labor difficulties in Cripple Creek. The labor conflict at Cripple Creek was very important in the history of western labor, and if he had a part in that conflict, it must have been insignificant. It is evident that he did not stay in Colorado because in the 1910 Census he was in Kansas as a schoolteacher. I cannot confirm admission to the Kansas bar. The census records indicate he was married with no children.

The Wyoming bar file shows that he was admitted as a lawyer on August 9, 1913. In his application, MacDougall listed his prior profession as "strike breaker." The Wyoming bar file also shows that he was living in the county poor house in 1913.[70] In March 1914, he handled a probate matter successfully. A young woman was wrongfully committed to the asylum in Colorado, and he managed to secure her release.[71] This is the first time he appeared as counsel in the *Westlaw* database.

There is no other record of him doing significant legal work prior to the Hill case. He showed up in Salt Lake City immediately before the trial. There is no explanation of why he moved to Salt Lake, as he clearly did not intend to abandon his Wyoming residence. Joe Hill said, "Well, there was this lawyer who came to me and said he was new in town, and that he would take my case without a fee." Elizabeth Gurley Flynn says, "He was a local socialist." The lawyer's experience appears limited, but the socialist part is true.

To confirm how long MacDougall had been in Salt Lake City, I contacted Pat Bartholomew, the clerk of the Utah Supreme Court.[72] The Utah Supreme Court maintains a roll of attorneys, and every new lawyer signs it. The Utah roll of attorneys has been maintained since territorial days. MacDougall signed the roll of Utah attorneys six days before the trial started.[73] So, he was, in fact, new in town.

Subsequent to the completion of the Joe Hill trial, MacDougall returned to Wyoming, where he stood for election as the Socialist candidate for justice of the Wyoming Supreme Court. He traveled Wyoming making speeches on behalf of socialism. He had little chance of electoral success given that the Progressives, Republicans, and Democrats agreed on a fusion candidate. That does not mean that MacDougall was a boring stump speaker.

> E. D. MacDougall of Cheyenne, Socialist candidate for Judge
> of the Supreme Court of Wyoming, addressed a meeting in

the Lyceum theatre last Thursday evening. A small crowd
was present, perhaps owing to other attractions, but it was
one of the best discussions of Socialism heard here in a long
time, and was well received.[74]

After his electoral defeat, he returned to Utah. He has a very sketchy
record in Salt Lake after the trial. He spoke before the Liberal Club on
March 19, 1915, complaining that the Utah legislature never did anything
for working men.[75] There is some record of him advertising his office
in the Boston Building but for a very short time. In 1915, he returned
to Wyoming to represent a Wyoming mining union against its former
secretary. The suit was for the return of embezzled funds. MacDougall
lost.[76] In its published opinion, the Wyoming court listed his residence as
Murray City, Utah.

In 1916, MacDougall went to the Uintah Basin representing the Duchesne
Land Company.[77] He was living in Myton. He was the socialist candidate
for district attorney of Duchesne County. He went all over the Uintah
Basin arguing about socialism. The Uintah Basin was the last area of Utah
settled by the Latter-day Saints. The land was opened for settlement only
after the Ute Indian Reservation was deliberately shrunk. The altitude
is high; the soil is poor. The people were conservative.[78] MacDougall
wore out his welcome. On March 10, 1917, the town of Myton[79] gave
MacDougall twenty-four hours to get out of town because they were tired
of him and his socialism. The townspeople accused MacDougall of being a
member of the IWW. MacDougall explained that he was not a member of
the IWW but only a socialist. This distinction was clear in MacDougall's
mind but lost upon the people, who ordered him from the town.[80]

MacDougall returned to Kansas. In the 1920 Census, he was again teaching
school but without a wife. We know he moved to Chicago by 1928. Again,
using *Westlaw*, we find him handling a few rather minor personal injury
cases. He had a specialty of suing Checker Cab for passengers injured on
exiting the car. As far as we can discover from *Westlaw*, MacDougall never
handled another criminal case.

In 1936, MacDougall wrote a book, *Speculation and Gambling*. He wrote
to all church leaders in the country, except the Mormons, and asked them

what their attitude was toward gambling. The major portion of the book is complaining of the inequity of grain speculation. Surprisingly, the book sold. He made money. Thereafter, MacDougall disappeared completely from the genealogical, legal, and historical record.

If a modern lawyer intends to handle a case when he is not experienced in the area of law, he can meet the competency requirements of Ethical Rule 1.1 by associating with experienced counsel. Who did MacDougall associate with? A fellow named Frank B. Scott.

Again, I don't have a picture because, although Frank B. Scott was rather notorious in Salt Lake City, it just doesn't exist. He was born in Nova Scotia. He went to college in Canada, where he affiliated with the socialists. So again, he was a Canadian socialist. He spent two years in the city attorney's office of Halifax, but he was in Salt Lake City by 1905.[81] He advertised quite heavily in the Salt Lake City newspapers, but he advertises that he was a "patent attorney." One would not expect a new and inexperienced lawyer, unfamiliar with the community, to engage a patent lawyer as cocounsel in the biggest murder trial in Utah.

Joe Hill called him a "shyster." Joe Hill was right. Frank Scott had a terrible business reputation. Again using *Westlaw*, we find that he was mired in heavy litigation by cheating people in a Montana mine before coming to Utah.[82] Scott had a coal mine fraud where he formed a corporation, and in spite of the fact that the coal mine did not exist, he sold the stock anyway.[83]

A few years before the Joe Hill case, he formed another corporation to buy a hotel. Somehow, he ended up with 60 percent of the stock, and the other shareholders sued him for fraud.[84]

He was a joiner. He was chairman of the Utah Socialist Party and introduced Eugene Debs when the presidential candidate visited Salt Lake City.[85] Scott came up with an idea for a food cooperative, which he promoted tirelessly.[86] He was also big in the Moose Lodge.[87] He formed the "Canadian" Club in Salt Lake City.[88]

In spite of these self-promoting ideas, he was a business failure. His name is found on the Millard County delinquent tax lists from 1908 to 1915. In 1926, there is a Utah case in which the state took custody of one of his grandchildren. The court noted, "F. B. Scott has no money to take care of this child."[89]

When the Depression started, he moved to Reno. He formed a law partnership with an imaginary lawyer whose made up name started with "AA," because the phone books were just coming out and he wanted to have the first listing. The Nevada court was not impressed with his phone book listing, but they were even less impressed with the fact that he represented both the husband and wife in a contested divorce. They disbarred him. There's a written opinion from Nevada. Again, according to the records maintained by Pat Bartholomew at the Utah Supreme Court, the Utah bar imposed reciprocal discipline, which means he also lost his Utah law license.[90]

MacDougall and Scott took the case for no money. The legal ethical rules preclude solicitation of clients, but this was not solicitation. A lawyer can ethically take a case for no money, but it is not recommended. In this case, taking the case for no money was deadly because MacDougall and Scott could have used money even if they refused personal payment.

If there ever was a case that cried out for money to hire an investigator, this was it. If Joe Hill wasn't going to tell what happened, the lawyers had to find witnesses who could have explained the gaps in time and behavior. If Joe Hill was to testify, MacDougall and Scott needed witnesses to firm up the testimony.

Regardless of Joe Hill's testimony, MacDougall and Scott needed to have witnesses to explain the alibi. More basically, they needed an investigator who could have talked to the eyewitnesses. It is clear from the appellate decisions and the news accounts that MacDougall and Scott went into this trial "cold," with no independent knowledge of what they could or could not expect from the Salt Lake witnesses.

What is more, if Joe Hill actually had a Luger and that Luger wasn't a .38 caliber and if he bought it from a Salt Lake City pawn shop, MacDougall and Scott needed an investigator to run down the information. The pawn shop clerk had moved to Chicago. If MacDougall and Scott had money, they could have sent an investigator to talk with the clerk.

MacDougall and Scott needed to investigate Joe Hill's pretrial conduct. The Salt Lake sheriff went to California to find out what there was to learn about Joe Hill, and he could not find anything.[91] Taking the case for no money really was a problem, but that's not where it ends. MacDougall and Scott quickly found themselves over their heads in a hotly contested trial. They were arrayed against Elmer Leatherwood, who although not Mormon was an experienced master of the Salt Lake legal atmosphere.

III

Ineffective Assistance of Counsel

It has often been charged that Hill received ineffective assistance of counsel. There are no cases from this period perhaps because there was not a constitutional right to have counsel in the first place. It is an axiom that if the defendant was entitled to a lawyer, he is not entitled to the best lawyer possible. Without a doubt, Clarence Darrow or Judge Hilton would have conducted better pretrial preparation and would have been able by education and experience to stand up to Elmer Leatherwood. But that was not the standard applied by the courts.

If we apply the federal constitutional standards developed twenty years after the Hill trial, it is hard to find that Joe Hill's defense was as ineffective as that of the Scottsboro boys. The special factors found by Justice Sutherland, particularly the hurried nature of the Georgia trial, simply are not there in Joe Hill's trial. Jury selection took the better part of a week and the actual trial longer than that. There is no evidence that MacDougall and Scott were threatened or harmed either during or after the trial. They were inexperienced, but Joe Hill knew that when he engaged MacDougall. I do not believe Justice Sutherland would have saved Joe Hill from his own error.

Joe Hill would have fared no better under modern Utah law on ineffective assistance of counsel. In *State v. Nelson-Waggoner*[92] the Utah Supreme

Court said that to prevail on a claim of ineffective assistance of counsel, the defendant would have to show both that counsel's performance was so deficient as to fall below an objective standard of reasonableness and that but for counsel's deficient performance there is a reasonable probability that the outcome would have been different. In Joe Hill's case, the lawyers may not have been the most skilled, but it is hard to prove that they were objectively incompetent. In any event, Hill would never have met the second prong given his refusal to provide alibi testimony in the face of the prosecutor's admissible evidence.

In Judge Hilton's disbarment case as well as the direct appeal, Justice Straup said that MacDougall made a number of evidentiary objections that were sustained by Judge Ritchie. There is no hint in either opinion that the Utah Supreme Court would have entertained an ineffective assistance argument. Indeed, Justice Straup says that to allow MacDougall and Scott to abandon Joe Hill in the trial would have been cruel. Given that Joe Hill was not entitled to a lawyer under then-existing Utah and federal law, Justice Straup is probably right that even MacDougall and Scott were better than nothing.

The fact that MacDougall and Scott were probably not guilty of ineffective assistance of counsel does not exonerate them from their inexperience and gross errors. Dr. Foner says that they were in contact with the IWW press as early as April. That is hard to reconcile with the evidence that MacDougall (clearly lead counsel) signed the roll of attorneys immediately prior to the opening of the trial. If MacDougall and Scott were in contact with the union prior to the trial and had time to properly prepare for trial, their failure to recognize their inexperience and to request help was grossly negligent.

I will argue that the proximate or immediate cause of losing this murder trial beyond the inherent difficulties of representing Joe Hill with his story in Salt Lake City was the overriding inexperience of MacDougall and Scott. It is beyond belief that everyone writing about this trial in the past has not considered the undisputable fact that MacDougall and Scott had very little idea of what they were doing in defending Joe Hill.

Law is not logic. Innocent people are convicted. Trial lawyers are not fungible. If Joe Hill had a defense, there was little chance that MacDougall and Scott had the ability to make a persuasive jury presentation. In concentrating on the unpopularity of the laboring class in Salt Lake City, Foner and Stavis miss the prime cause of this disastrous trial result.

Chapter 6

A Difficult Case and a Difficult Client

Truth is tough. It will not break like a bubble, at the touch, nay, you
may kick it about all day like a football and it will be round and full
at evening.

Certitude is not the test of certainty. We have been cocksure of many
things that were not so.

Justice Oliver Wendell Holmes

The great trial lawyer Gerry Spence teaches, "Everything in life is a story."
A trial is a contest between two competing stories.[93] To succeed at trial,
the lawyer must tell a more compelling story. A very good Alaskan lawyer,
Rick Friedman, explains the problem this way.

> And that's what trials are about—competing stories. You have
> your story of what happened; the defense has theirs. Which
> is more believable to the jury? Which is more compelling
> because it fits with the jurors' life experience?
>
> At trial, you need to answer questions. What happened?
> Why did it happen? Why did the people involved act as
> they did? Are they good, responsible people? Irresponsible?
> Why is this case important? Why should a juror care about

the case? How could this case affect me or my community?
All of these questions will be on the minds of jurors as the
trial opens and as the two sides battle for whose story grabs
the jurors.[94]

At the beginning of the Joe Hill case, the lawyers had to decide what
story they would tell the jury. There was evidence in Joe Hill's favor.
The authorities never found the bullet that went through his body. The
evidence that the Morrison gun was even fired was equivocal. There were
no definite eyewitnesses. There was no evidence of animosity between
Joe Hill and the murdered Mr. Morrison. There was nothing taken in the
robbery. There was no evidence of motive whatsoever.

What story could be told? The obvious story would be a failure of proof.
With dedication and effort, the defense lawyers might have been able
to demonstrate that the witnesses were either confused or did not have
the opportunity to observe. The defense could attack the notion that
the Morrison gun was fired. Motive was undercut by the failure to steal
anything and the probable fact that Joe Hill never met Mr. Morrison in
his life. This is a beguiling story.

To the inexperienced lawyer or an inexperienced observer, it seems more
compelling than perhaps it was. There is evidence the lawyers simply
could not make go away. All the defense lawyers both at trial and on
appeal thought that they could keep evidence of Joe Hill's wound from
the jury. It is hard to articulate a legal strategy or compelling story that did
not begin with exclusion of the wound and the alibi.

Yet, exclusion of the fact that Joe Hill was shot was almost impossible.
If we were looking at exclusion of the wound today, the lawyers would
have to grapple with Evidence Rule 401 admissibility.[95] Under evidence
rules today or evidence rules in 1914, the standard to be applied by Judge
Ritchie is if it is probable that the wound tells the jury something about
the identity of the robber. The relevance and admissibility of evidence of
the wound is a low standard. It would be nearly impossible to convince
the trial judge that the wound was not in some way relevant to identity.
Certainly on appeal, Justice Straup found that it had great relevance. If
you could not convince the trial court that the wound had no relevance,

you would be left with the equivalent of an Evidence Rule 403[96] argument that the introduction of evidence of the wound was more prejudicial than it was probative.

Certainly, telling the jury that Joe Hill had been shot the night of the assault was prejudicial, but was it unfairly prejudicial? The answer to that question depends upon circumstances. How close in time was the wound? How far from the Morrison store was the doctor's office? Could a person with Joe Hill's wound walk that far? Was there evidence that Joe Hill was transported? The answers to such questions may have brought the relevance of the wound into question and planted doubt in the mind of the judge. If the evidence was submitted to the jury, those questions might have raised reasonable doubt.

The lawyers would also have to discern a manner to deal with the other major evidentiary matter, which was Joe Hill's alibi. That alibi is the elephant in the room. The jurors are going to want an explanation of that alibi. If the trial lawyers could not keep the alibi out of evidence, they had a real problem. There had to be a reasonable explanation for the alibi. Jurors do not like loose ends, nor do they like an attorney telling lies. The lawyers handling this case of necessity had to develop a reasonable story for the alibi.

Those evidentiary matters control how the case should have been handled. At trial, no effort was made to exclude the evidence. On appeal, Joe Hill's lawyers argued that the evidence was irrelevant. Without an effort at trial to exclude the wound and the alibi, the case became difficult, if not problematic. Justice Straup called the alibi "weird and vague." Without a compelling story to the contrary, it is hard to see how the jurors thought otherwise.

In telling the story, the defense lawyers had to make Joe Hill sympathetic to the Salt Lake jury. This was difficult because Joe Hill was a difficult client. Joe Hill was dedicated to his art. He was also fully engaged in labor arguments. He never lost the gift of memorable language. Two weeks before his execution, he told the press that he was going to Mars to organize the canal workers for the IWW.[97] I thought about how to describe just how difficult Joe Hill would have been to present to a Salt

Lake jury. Beyond the normal problems of generating sympathy from the jury, Joe Hill had well-defined political agenda and class that he would not abandon. This makes him a doubly difficult client. Not only must the lawyer tell his story, but he must also make the jury want to vote for acquittal. Difficult clients complicate the lawyer's life and make the story more difficult. It is impossible to find a more difficult client for Salt Lake City than Joe Hill.

Joe Hill's songs are the best illustrations of the difficulty faced by MacDougall and Scott. Consider trying a case with trying this case with Joe Hill's views in 1914 Utah.

There Is Power in a Union

There is power, there is power
In a band of workingmen
When they stand, hand to hand,
There's a power, there's a power
That must rule every land
One Industrial Union Grand.

Come all you workers from every land
Come join the great industrial band.
Then we our share of this earth shall demand.
Come on! Do your share like a man.

Now how would a lawyer defend a client in 1914 Utah who had that opinion about unions? I think that lawyer would be behind the power curve. The strike at Bingham Canyon was settled eighteen months before the murder, and the miners were not Mormon.Now, if you don't think our hypothetical lawyer was behind the curve with that song, try this one. This is his most famous song. This is the *Preacher and the Slave*. It's where he coins the term "pie in the sky." Listen to how Joe Hill talks about religion.

[Music—Joe Hill was a union organizer in the USA who was murdered by the forces of reaction. This song deals with the needs of working people then and now for a better life now and not after death.]

Preacher and the Slave

Long haired preachers come out every night,
Try to tell you what's wrong and what's right;
But when asked about something to eat
They will answer with voices so sweet.

(Chorus)
You will eat, bye and bye,
In that glorious land above the sky;
Work and pray, live on hay,
You'll get pie in the sky when you die.

The Starvation Army they play,
They sing and the clap and they pray,
Till they get all your coin on the drum,
Then they tell you when you're on the bum.

If you fight hard for children and wife—
Try to get something good in this life
You're a sinner and bad man they tell,
When you die you will sure go to hell.

Workingmen of all countries, unite,
Side by Side we for freedom will fight;
When the world and its wealth we have gained
To the grafters we sing this refrain.

You will eat, bye and bye,
In that glorious land above the sky;
Work and pray, live on hay,
You'll get pie in the sky when you die.

It's a lie.

How would a lawyer explain that man's view of religion in Mormon
Utah? Joe Hill, like most of the IWW leadership, was atheist or at least

agnostic. Justice Straup was a Unitarian, but he was vastly outnumbered by Mormons who believed in continuing revelation. Even the non-Mormons of Salt Lake City were on the whole practicing Christians of a conservative bent.

The problem is even worse. Utah had fought great battles over the structure of marriage, but no one believed that marriage was inappropriate. Joe Hill, of course, never married. Further, his view of the place of women in society was as labor organizers. While Joe Hill was in jail, Elizabeth Gurley Flynn, who was an IWW organizer, founder of the ACLU, and an early communist, visited him. He wrote a song about her called "The Rebel Girl."

Elizabeth Gurley Flynn: It wasn't long after those big strikes in the east, the Patterson and the Lawrence strike, that there was a great strike of copper workers in the state of Utah. It was there that Joe Hill, I'm sure that all of you have heard of Joe Hill, the songwriter, the troubadour of the IWW, was arrested. The little red songbook that never died, apparently anymore than the memory of Joe Hill, has many of his songs.

If there is one thing that I am really proud of in my long labor history, it is that that while he was in prison, before he was executed, he wrote a song dedicated to me that was called "The Rebel Girl." That song, I hope you do hear it sometime. It may not be the best of words or the best of music, but it came from the heart and it was so treasured.

[Song] Rebel Girl

There are women of many descriptions,
In this queer world as everyone knows,
Some are living in beautiful mansions,
And wearing the finest of clothes.
There are blue-blooded queens and princesses,
Who have charms made of diamonds and pearls,
But the only and thoroughbred lady
Is the Rebel Girl.

(chorus)

She's the rebel girl, she's the rebel girl
To the working class she's a precious pearl
She brings courage and pride, to fight by your side
And I'm proud to fight for freedom
With the Rebel Girl.

Yes, her hands may be hardened from labor,
And her dress may not be very fine;
But a heart in her bosom is beating
That is true to her class and her kind
For the only and thoroughbred lady,
Is the Rebel Girl.

Joe Hill had a well-developed philosophy long before he came to Utah. That philosophy did not change, even when he was in jail facing execution. Any lawyer handling this case would have to realize that Joe Hill was not going to change his beliefs. The lawyer would have to realize that he was dealing with beliefs foreign to Salt Lake City, and the defense would need to be constructed in accordance with Hill's beliefs. For example, I think it unlikely from the beginning that Hill could have ever been convinced to testify on his own behalf.

II

What Story to Tell?

This trial can be viewed from top down. The jury was told a story about a wandering labor man who looked like the thief and had a wound consistent with a wound received in the Morrison store. The jury was told a story about a man with an unbelievable alibi. The jury heard this story from Elmer Leatherwood. He was a methodical man with deliberate speech who built his case witness upon witness.

The opposing story that Joe Hill was an innocent victim of circumstance was never convincingly told. The jury was not convinced that the authorities were picking on Joe Hill. This story might have been convincing to some of the Mormon jurors given the long Mormon fight with authority. It just was not told.

Looking at the trial from this vantage point, the result does not seem unusual. To move the jury past the wound, the alibi, and the client would have required experienced lawyers. It would have taken great creativity. It would have taken weeks and long days of preparation. It would have taken serious investigation of the prosecution witnesses. It would have taken an effort to find witnesses to bolster the alibi. However, it might have been accomplished.

The story of Joe Hill's trial is sad. It was not a credit to the profession. A good, perhaps even a great, lawyer may have lost this case. A good or great lawyer would have told the jury a story that, in the absence of other proof, might have been believed. Evaluation of the case is where this trial fiasco began.

Chapter 7

A Man Named Kimball

Most of the things we do, we do for no better reason than that our fathers have done them or our neighbors do them and the same is true of a larger part than we suspect of what we think

Justice Oliver Wendell Holmes

I

The Great American Jury

The American trial jury is of ancient origin. It arose in the early middle ages in England. Originally, the jury was not constituted of impartial judges but of men who actually witnessed the crime or injury. By the time of the American settlement, an impartial jury had become a fixture in what were viewed as traditional rights of Englishmen. In colonial times, there were famous jury trials such as the acquittal of John Peter Zenger on libel charges in New York City.

Two of the most important Boston patriots were noted for their courtroom presence. John Adams long remembered James Otis' argument against Writs of Assistance, which would have allowed searches without probable cause. Adams said that it was then and there that American independence was born.

Adams himself demonstrated remarkable trial skills, of which he was justly proud. Adams was lead counsel in the trial of Captain Thomas Preston, who was accused in the Boston massacre. None of the labor lawyers ever faced a more hostile community than prerevolutionary Boston. Yet Adams prevailed. Reading accounts of the trial, one realizes that Adams was able to appeal to the jury's sense of fairness and justice after telling a coherent story.

Among the chief complaints by colonial Americans against Great Britain was the infringement of jury trials. Massachusetts smugglers feared Admiralty Courts because there were no juries. In the Declaration of Independence, Thomas Jefferson indicted King George, "For depriving us, in many cases, of the benefits of trial by jury." When the Bill of Rights was adopted, Amendment Six protected the right of a "speedy and public trial by an impartial jury ..." Additionally, the Seventh Amendment protected the right to jury trials in civil cases.

The American jury has been celebrated in movies. Henry Fonda's performance in the 1957 version of *Twelve Angry Men* demonstrates in popular culture the importance of jurors speaking their minds and remaining firm to their convictions. The American Bar Association found that the best lawyer movie of all time was *To Kill a Mockingbird* with its memorable performance by Gregory Peck. Paul Newman played a sleazy plaintiff's lawyer in *The Verdict*. Tom Cruise played the defense lawyer in *A Few Good Men*. Other movies include *The Caine Mutiny*. It is clear that juries and jury lawyers are deep within the American consciousness.

II

Error in Jury Trials

I believe in juries. In a civilized world, we need a method of resolving disputes. In an ever more complex world, the notion that disputes should be submitted to the collective wisdom of the community is comforting. The medical profession believes that medical disputes are beyond such wisdom and should be removed from jury consideration. The tort reformers believe that juries may be swayed into multimillion dollar judgments on frivolous cases. Yet in my experience, almost every jury member takes his or her responsibility seriously and tries very hard to reach a just result.

I am not certain that there is a better system. There is a much higher rate of conviction in cases tried only to a judge. Joe Hill would not have had a chance if his case was tried to Judge Morris Ritchie. Even in civil cases, there is a great sense of democracy when submitting causes to a panel of ordinary citizens. I tell younger lawyers that they must learn to trust their jury because on the whole juries get things right.

Those of us who have practiced before juries know that there is a rate of failure. We know that juries make mistakes. No one can prove the rate of failure scientifically, because in human experience, there is no such thing as absolute truth. The relevant question in the Joe Hill matter is, "How much error will society accept?"

It is clear that society accepts much less error, particularly in death penalty cases, today than it did at the turn of the twentieth century. In June 2010, Utah executed Ronnie Lee Gardner for murder. Associate Chief Justice Durrant of the Utah Supreme Court explained how carefully the court system had reviewed each and every claim raised on behalf of Gardner.

> Review of Mr. Gardner's case has been ongoing for nearly twenty-five years, during which time great caution and care have been exercised by multiple courts in order to safeguard his rights. In that time, Mr. Gardner has appeared before this court six times. Given the facts of this case, all of the procedures Mr. Gardner has had an opportunity to invoke, and the nature of the claims he raises now, we are satisfied that no injustice will result from our decision not to resolve his petition based on the merits of his claims.[98]

Joe Hill got one appeal and three appearances before the commutation board. The time between conviction and execution was one year and five months. Society in 1915 was simply willing to accept much more risk in the execution of the accused than it is today.[99]

In Joe Hill's case, there are too many questions as to guilt to justify imposition of a death sentence. As we will see, if this case were tried today, there would be a significant ineffective assistance of counsel motion, followed by federal habeas proceedings. Given what we know of the Joe Hill record, reasonable counsel could have kept Joe Hill alive longer than Gardner. Further, there is a good chance counsel would have succeeded in the post-conviction proceedings and obtained Joe Hill the new trial he sought.

III

Mormons and Jury Trials

Mormons had distinctly bad experiences with jury trials, particularly those influenced by non-Mormons. Dallin H. Oaks is a church apostle. Prior to his church calling, he taught at the University of Chicago Law School, was president of Brigham Young University, and was a Utah Supreme Court Justice. In collaboration with Mormon historian Marvin Hill, Oaks wrote a book on the trials of the murderers of the Mormon Prophet Joseph Smith. *Carthage Conspiracy* is largely devoted to the doctrine of "jury nullification." This means that the jury decides that an individual is not guilty regardless of the instruction of law given by the judge.[100] In the case of the Smith mob, no one was convicted.

Nineteenth-century Mormons were well aware of jury nullification, as it was often used to justify murdering Mormons. Popular apostle Parley P. Pratt was murdered in Arkansas in 1857. His killer went unpunished by the courts. On two occasions in the Utah period, Mormon missionaries were murdered in the Southern states with juries refusing to punish the guilty. On July 21, 1878, Elder Joseph Standing was murdered in Georgia, with all assailants found not guilty on all counts. On August 10, 1884, two elders and two church investigators were killed by a mob at Cane Creek, Tennessee. Again, the jury system failed the Latter-day Saints.

Even in Utah, the Latter-day Saints had reason to distrust the jury system. In the crusade against polygamy, many Latter-day Saint men were disfranchised by a test oath and thus eliminated from the jury pool.

Further, federal officials in the territory actively sought to eliminate Mormons from the jury pool and thus manipulate justice.

This is most evident in the Engelbrecht fiasco. The Latter-day Saint police in Salt Lake City raided a liquor establishment that had been repeatedly fined for violation of the law. The defendant repeatedly appealed to the federally controlled judiciary, which threw out the convictions. Finally, the defendants filed a civil action against the Latter-day Saint police officers alleging destruction of property.

Territorial law provided for calling jury members by the county clerk. This would result in a large majority of Mormon jury panel members. An openly hostile non-Mormon judge overruled this procedure. Claiming that his court was not a territorial court but a federal court, he ordered the United States marshall to select the jurymen from non-Mormons.

Objection having been made to this extraordinary effort to exclude Latter-day Saints from the jury, appeal was taken to the United States Supreme Court. Chief Justice Waite refused to engage in Mormon politics. His opinion rests solely on a discussion of congressional intent to allow local control of juries in the territories of the United States. He cited precedent originating in the Northwest Ordinance indicating that it was improper for federal officials to override local control of juries.[101]

The Joe Hill jury had this legacy of outside challenge to Mormon domination of juries or even exclusion of Mormons from jury service. The Hill jury was not homogenous. It had eight baptized Mormons and four non-Mormons. Six of twelve were foreign born. There was a variety of occupations. This divergence made no difference because the foreman of the jury was well indoctrinated into Mormon views and grievances.

IV

Mysterious Jury Selection

Elmer Leatherwood was the district attorney, non-Mormon, educated at the University of Wisconsin law school. He came to Utah after polygamy.[102] He became a Republican congressman from Utah for about fifteen years.

Leatherwood proved to be a very able attorney. He was also familiar with the Salt Lake County population and was cognizant of the Mormon and non-Mormon divides. Leatherwood made no mistakes in trial procedure. In particular, he made no mistakes in jury selection. He knew exactly who was and was not in the jury pool.

MacDougall and Scott were incompetent in jury selection. We can discern this weakness from the newspapers, sources Dr. Foner cites, as well as language in the appellate decision. Judge Ritchie used lawyer-conducted *voir dire*. This is the process by which lawyers or the court question prospective jury members. I am ambiguous on how I feel about lawyer-conducted *voir dire* as opposed to questioning by the judge. I know there are lawyers who feel like they want to control their case by questioning the prospective jurors themselves. They do not want the judge getting between them and "their" jury.

In Alaska, all *voir dire* is conducted by the attorneys. I can tell you as a young attorney in that system what happens. The inexperienced lawyers don't use *voir dire* for the two legitimate reasons, which are: 1) to see if someone's challengeable for cause (ineligible to sit on the jury for legal reasons), and 2) to intelligently use your preemptory challenges. Preemptory challenges may be used by each side to dismiss a prospective juror for any reason the lawyers choose. What inexperienced attorneys do and what I did and what I had to learn not to do is spend your time trying to propagandize the jury. That is what was going on in the Joe Hill case. MacDougall and Scott did not ask questions that would disclose the prospective juror's background. Instead they attempted to commit the prospective juror to their point of view.

Dr. Foner cites an instance where MacDougall and Scott questioned a juror for three hours, repeatedly asking about the presumption of innocence and burden of proof. Finally, the judge cut it off and got mad at them. Dr. Foner says, "That shows evidence of bias." What it shows to me, having been in that situation, is the judge got tired of their attempt to propagandize the jury. If you read the Supreme Court's decision, you'll see that cutting off *voir dire* questioning of prospective jurors was one of the minor points on appeal. The Utah Supreme Court said it was not error. "Cutting off repeated questioning was within the trial judge's discretion."

The court was following a method of seating the jury not in use today. It's called "strike and replace." The judge would call one juror at a time to the jury box. Both sides would question the prospective juror. They could challenge the juror "for cause," again meaning that there were legal reasons to excuse the juror. Then they would exercise their preemptory challenge to that juror. If he was excused, then the judge would call another juror to the box. Because the Joe Hill court used "strike and replace," we know the order that jurors were seated.

It is clear from the news accounts that Judge Morris Ritchie[103] was having a terrible time getting a jury. The *Salt Lake Herald* said, "They went through numerous jury panels." The news accounts don't tell us how big those jury panels were. In fact, the transcript for the first half of the trial went missing somewhere around 1930, so we do not know exactly how many jurors were questioned.

Even though we do not know the exact number of jurors questioned, we do know that jury selection took the better part of a week. It is apparent from the news articles that the prosecutor was not challenging jurors for cause, nor was Leatherwood using his preemptory challenges on prospective jurors. In accounting for the large number of prospective jurors, we have to conclude that Judge Ritchie was excusing jurors for cause pretty freely. In other words, Judge Ritchie was not trying to force a particular jury on Joe Hill and his lawyers. Further, the defense lawyers were trying to get a particular type of juror because it is clear that MacDougall and Scott used all of their preemptory challenges. We know that to be true because they complained about not having more.[104]

Joe Hill told a story about how when Judge Ritchie was trying to get his jury, eight men who had been on a previous jury whose jury term had not expired came into the courtroom. Judge Ritchie said, "Get in here. You're sitting for this case too." [105] One of them became the jury foreman. But no one, not Joe Hill, MacDougall and Scott, or any of the writers, knew the identity of this man. Joe Hill said his name was Kimball, and he was an old man. The papers disclose that Kimball was the second or third juror seated. Thus MacDougall and Scott had plenty of preemptory challenges left when he was seated. The fact that they did not use a preemptory challenge meant that MacDougall and Scott wanted Kimball on their jury. If MacDougall and Scott had thought there to be something wrong with Kimball serving, they had ample opportunity to remedy the situation. Using their stock questions about burden of proof and presumption of innocence, MacDougall and Scott did not discover the character, experience, or biases of Kimball.

In fact, Joseph Smith Kimball was an old man. He was born in 1851, and he was by twenty years the oldest man on the jury. The real question that neither the trial lawyers nor the Joe Hill historians accounted for is, "Who was Joseph Smith Kimball?" For that answer, I have to take you deep into Mormon history.

Joseph Smith, the founder of the LDS Church, recorded a revelation on plural marriages as early as 1832. But he did not practice polygamy until the Latter Day Saints removed to Nauvoo, Illinois, in 1843. At that point, he sealed himself or was married to a great number of women.

The second and third women he married in polygamy were Prescinda and Zina Huntington. The Huntington family were some of the first converts to the LDS Church. The father, William Huntington, was prominent enough that he is mentioned in the LDS Doctrine and Covenants as a member of the Nauvoo Stake High Council.[106] The brothers, Dimick and Oliver, were prominent enough in the early church period, including the Utah period, that the twentieth-century criminal Mark Hoffman forged their signatures and sold the document to the LDS Church. In fact, Dimick brought Joseph Smith's body to Nauvoo after his assassination.[107]

Prescinda and Zina were in their midtwenties when sealed to Joseph. After Joseph died, most of the women who had been sealed to him in polygamist marriages were sealed for life to the surviving apostles. Zina was sealed to Brigham Young. Prescinda was married to apostle Heber C. Kimball.

Prescinda had two children with Heber C. Kimball. The death of her first Kimball child is a sad story. The child was a little girl who was also named Prescinda. When settlers arrived in the valley, the child was three years old. The child wandered off and drowned in City Creek. In 1851, Prescinda gave birth to the man known as Joseph Smith Kimball who became the foreman of the Joe Hill jury.[108]

Joseph Kimball was closely connected to the LDS Church leadership. Of course, everyone in Mormon Utah knew that he was sealed to Joseph. The biological father, Herber C. Kimball, was the second most important apostle in the Utah period. His wife was the daughter of apostle Orson Pratt. His maternal aunt, Zina Huntington was president of the women's organization called the Relief Society.

At the time of the trial, his brother J. Golden Kimball was a general authority of the Church.[109] His nephew, Orson F. Whitney, was an apostle. His sister was married to Church president Joseph F. Smith. Joseph Kimball had a twenty-year-old nephew, future Church president Spencer W. Kimball,[110] who was knocking on doors as a young missionary in St. Louis. Joseph Kimball was well connected to church leadership. When Church president Wilford Woodruff died, Joseph Kimball was on the committee that arranged the funeral. Joseph Kimball and his wife were the first official guides on Temple Square in Salt Lake City.

His personal life is even more interesting than his church connections. As a young man, he was called by Brigham Young to settle Rich County. He became quite wealthy in the ranching business. He invested in mines and irrigation companies. He served twenty-eight years as LDS bishop in Rich County. He moved to Logan, served as bishop there for about eight more years. He founded the Logan Chamber of Commerce.

The failure to conduct proper jury questioning gets worse than the failure to discover church connections and leadership. Joseph Kimball's political activity includes two terms in the territory legislature. Kimball served in the Utah Constitutional Convention and served another two terms in the state legislature. He was a member of the Sons of the American Revolution.

It is hard to imagine why Joseph Kimball would have natural sympathy with the labor songwriter. It is even harder to imagine why MacDougall and Scott did not discover any or all of this information in questioning Kimball.[111]

There are a lot of schools of thought about how a lawyer should exercise his preemptory challenges. There was a lawyer in Alaska, a very successful criminal trial lawyer, Edgar Paul Boyco,[112] who gave a seminar on how to pick a jury by using horoscopes. If you read trial literature, it will tell the novice lawyer all kinds of things. Don't put Presbyterians on the jury. Don't put Methodists on the jury either.

I cannot see how any of that trial advocacy advice makes much sense. My law firm shows a mock courtroom on television. That mock courtroom is not only an advertising device. We mock try a lot of cases. We do a lot of focus groups in there. We are trying to discover which potential jurors will respond favorably to our clients and our clients' stories. Selecting a proper jury is not always inherently easy. We find many anomalies. Cases that we think will appeal to a particular jury person sometimes appeal to persons with more or less education. My experience is that the only thing a lawyer can intelligently do with his preemptory challenges in jury selection is get rid of the outliers. These are the individuals with strong opinions who are not likely to be persuaded under any circumstances. They are the individuals who are likely to have inordinate influence with the other members of the jury.

I cannot think of any valid reason why MacDougall and Scott would not have gotten rid of Joseph Kimball. I would not want someone from the Constitutional Convention sitting on a murder jury. I would not want an older, successful businessman sitting with a younger jury. In Utah, I would not want someone connected to Church leadership the way Kimball was because such individuals have the tendency to dominate discussion.

This is not religious bias. The trial lawyer must bring the jury along with his explanation of the case step by step. It is not a good idea to have a person like Kimball on the jury whose personal authority might supersede that of the attorney. But MacDougall and Scott could not intelligently use their preemptory challenge on Kimball because they did not ask the right questions. They were not asking questions that would tell them who this person was and what he had done in his life. They were still trying to propagandize the jury. They never discovered his identity then or later.

MacDougall and Scott seemed oblivious to the Mormon makeup of their jury. From the remaining records, most importantly news accounts and the appellate opinions, we find no evidence that they even asked the questions about church service and leadership. I would want to know if Kimball had been bishop. I think that fact would inform me about the desirability of exercising a preemptory challenge. I think it would have been reasonable to consult *Pioneers and Prominent Men of Utah* to see if a person of Kimball's age was listed.

MacDougall was a total stranger to the community. One would expect Frank Scott to have at least been cognizant of the Mormon pioneer issue. Clarence Darrow or Judge Hilton would not have been ignorant.

I have had trials where the outcome was determined in jury selection.[113] This was not necessarily the case with Joe Hill. The fact remains that MacDougall and Scott began their presentation with a heavy burden. That burden was not the fault of either the "copper bosses" or the Mormon Church. It was the result of gross incompetence of the trial lawyers selecting their jury.

The left side of Joe Hill's face showing scars

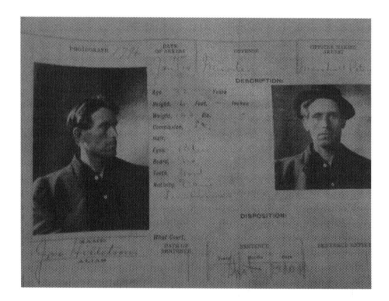

Joseph Kimball

Joseph Kimball with His Mother Prescinda Huntington Smith Kimball
Courtesy of Daughters of Utah Pioneers

Prescinda Celeste Kimball sister of Joseph Kimball
Courtesy of Daughters of Utah Pioneers

Vincent St. John

Elizabeth Gurley Flynn

William (Bill) Haywood

ILLINOIS.—PORTRAITS OF THE CONDEMNED CHICAGO ANARCHISTS.
FROM ORIGINAL PHOTOS. BY BEUTELL.—NEW YORK CITY.

The Haymarket Martyrs

Governor William Spry

Dr. James E. Talmage

B.H. Roberts

Joseph F. Smith

Senator Frank J. Cannon

Heber C. Kimball

Joseph Smith, Jr.

Justice Oliver Wendell Holmes

The Prosecutor Elmer Leatherwood

The Trial Judge, Morris Ritchie

Chief Justice Daniel Straup

Orrin N. Hilton

Frank Nebeker

Charles Varion

Attorney General Albert Barnes

Clarence Darrow in 1905

Chapter 8

A Litany of Error

This is a court of law, young man, and not a court of justice.

Justice Oliver Wendell Holmes

I

Was the Trial Legal?

Only a staunch revisionist with law and order beliefs would claim the Joe Hill trial to have been error free. In fact, the handling of the case was replete with error. Any trial lawyer who reads the Utah Supreme Court opinions will not miss the amateur approach of MacDougall and Scott. Trial error is the primary reason it is impossible to evaluate actual innocence or guilt.

Trial error does not mean that the jury decision should be reversed. In most instances, the errors were errors of bad judgment by MacDougall. An error in judgment (such as putting Joseph Kimball on the jury) is not an error of law. The question considered by the Utah court in 1915 was not whether the trial could have been handled in a better manner by more experienced counsel. The question was not whether the case was "fair." The question was, "Were the procedural and legal rules followed by the trial court?" Certainly, the appellate inquiry had nothing to do with the question of Joe Hill's innocence.[114]

Further, the 1915 Utah Supreme Court was not conducting an independent investigation into questions of constitutionality or law that might arise in the subsequent century. It was only obliged to answer questions actually brought to its attention as possible error by Joe Hill's lawyers.

With those understandings, the trial errors of MacDougall and Scott become perhaps the most important element of the Joe Hill matter. It is impossible to exaggerate how badly this case was handled at trial, but it was badly handled within the rules of trial procedure. The blame for this result rests not upon the "copper bosses," the Mormon Church, the judicial system, or any other conspiracy. It cannot be blamed on the prosecutor or the judge.

In sum, MacDougall and Scott sealed Joe Hill's fate, and they did it to their client and themselves.

II

A Man with Scars

Joe Hill contracted a form of tuberculosis called *Scrofula*. He was treated for this disease at a Stockholm hospital. The infection settled in the lymph nodes at approximately the angle of the jaw. In preantibiotic days, the treatment was to either drain the nodes or cut them out entirely. In Joe Hill's case, this surgery left him with noticeable scarring on the left side of his face and nose.[115] This scarring is not noticeable in the existing pictures of Joe Hill until the picture is enlarged. When enlarged, the scarring is noticeable. MacDougall and Scott's most glaring and fundamental errors of trial practice concern this easily seen scarring. The matter is of fundamental importance and cannot be lightly ignored.

Joe Hill had no lawyer at the preliminary hearing. A preliminary hearing is held to see if there is sufficient evidence to believe that a crime has been committed and that there is evidence linking the accused to the crime. The state's burden of proof is to put on some evidence supporting its theory of the case. The state need not prove guilt beyond a reasonable doubt at the preliminary hearing.

At Joe Hill's preliminary hearing, a number of witnesses testified as to the appearance of the robber. None mentioned scarring on the left side of Joe Hill's face and nose. All testified that their view of the assailant was at night in varying conditions of light. By the time the case came to trial, several of the witnesses had recovered a recollection of a man with prominent scars.

This situation calls for skill in what lawyers call "impeachment." It was incumbent upon MacDougall and Scott to show that the testimony of the witnesses had changed. It was also incumbent upon the lawyers to demonstrate that this changed testimony was unlikely to be true based upon the witnesses' perception particularly because of lighting. This did not happen. MacDougall and Scott simply let the witnesses get away with changing their story.

A transcript of the preliminary testimony was made. It has since disappeared, but Joe Hill had a copy. Joe Hill had the transcript memorized. He knew that the evidence put on by the prosecutor was not the same. He knew that no one testified at the preliminary hearing that they had seen a man with scarring on his neck. In this respect, Joe Hill had a better perspective than his lawyers.

There are two possible reasons why this failure to impeach the prosecution witnesses happened. I do not think MacDougall and Scott were prepared to effectively impeach these witnesses. Proper preparation would have required diligent study of the preliminary hearing transcript. A lawyer cannot use prior sworn testimony to impeach if he does not have that testimony committed to memory. This takes days and even weeks of study. I do not know how MacDougall and Scott could have been prepared in the short time they had before the trial. There is no evidence MacDougall and Scott even knew the importance of the changed testimony. From the arguments that later appeared in the *Salt Lake Telegram*, it is doubtful that MacDougall and Scott even knew that the testimony had changed.

The evidence that MacDougall and Scott were not prepared to meet the changed testimony of the eyewitnesses is overwhelming. In fact, Hill was sitting at counsel table, pointing to the transcript, and saying, "Look. Look. Look," and Scott was telling him, "Shut up, you look guilty." It drove Joe Hill crazy, as well it should. Preparation for impeachment is the most basic of trial responsibilities.

The other reason for the failure to significantly impeach the identification testimony was MacDougall and Scott did not have the skill to know how to pin the witnesses to their prior testimony. Impeaching a hostile witness is not inherently easy. I know it took me a number of years to learn how to impeach a hostile witness. A foundation must be laid for the prior testimony. The witness must testify in a contrary manner. The changed testimony must be highlighted for the jury.

MacDougall and Scott failed to demonstrate the necessary skills. Looking at the cases they handled, they never demonstrated such skills either before or after the trial. It seems obvious to me that Joe Hill was watching lawyers do their very first important case. It may well have been MacDougall's first trial of any sort.

I learned trial work by trying cases. Most of the time there was little at stake beyond the insurance company's money. MacDougall and Scott thought they could learn to try a case by taking on the most important murder trial in Utah history. The mistakes they made in failing to impeach the eyewitnesses are the mistakes of a young lawyer. With time, effort, and guidance, MacDougall and Scott probably would have improved their technique. They were learning on the job at Joe Hill's expense.

The failure of experience was an error that went uncorrected. In this respect, the trial was unfair to Joe Hill's case. Judge Ritchie was not at the preliminary hearing. He was listening to the testimony for the first time. He would have had no way of knowing about witness testimony discrepancies. If one is convinced of a conspiracy, one might surmise that Elmer Leatherwood suborned perjury through influence on the witnesses. But catching suborned perjury was the job of MacDougall and Scott.

The changed testimony did not even have to be perjury. The witnesses might have been sincere. They might have come to believe their changed stories. It does not matter. MacDougall and Scott failed their client at the most important time in the trial. Without the evidence that someone resembling Joe Hill was at the scene, the only evidence tying him to the crime was his wound and his alibi. No one can tell for certain that elementary impeachment would have changed the outcome. But it would have been a start in the right direction.

III

The Lawyers are Fired

Ultimate control of a legal case rests with the client. The lawyer's task is to advocate his client's case. The lawyer is to do so within the bounds of ethics and in obedience to the law. The lawyer may make decisions on tactics, but those decisions are always subordinate to the overall control of the case. The lawyer may decide how to present a particular argument, but in the end it is the client who has to live with the consequences, and the lawyer is bound to respect those wishes.[116]

To be effective, a lawyer must have the confidence of his client. To keep that confidence, the lawyer must communicate and discuss all material aspects of the case so the client is fully informed. The Rules of Professional Responsibility require that the lawyer advocate vigorously for his client. The client has the right to look to his lawyer not only for advice but also for loyalty.

MacDougall and Scott lost the confidence of Joe Hill. In his letter to the newspapers, Joe Hill is explicit about why he lost confidence in his lawyers. Not surprisingly, it was because MacDougall and Scott did not cross-examine the witnesses. Joe Hill knew what was supposed to happen, and MacDougall and Scott did not perform.

Joe Hill finally had enough of their incompetence. He blew up and said, "There are three lawyers in this courtroom, and they're all trying to convict me. That's two lawyers too many." He fired MacDougall and Scott on the spot. One of the news accounts says that MacDougall left the courtroom immediately but Scott remained.

Judge Ritchie did send the jury out before proceeding with inquiry into Joe Hill's mind. The judge did exactly what you would find in a modern case. He asked about Joe Hill's mental state. He asked if he'd been under the influence of any intoxicants. He asked him if he understood what he was taking on by self-representation. He went through the whole litany that you'd find in a modern case. Joe Hill answered affirmatively, but then, he hired MacDougall and Scott back that afternoon. In the second half of the trial, you have both the lawyers and Joe Hill questioning witnesses.

Gibbs Smith and others assign as error the trial court's actions when Joe Hill "fired his attorneys." They think that Judge Ritchie should have declared a mistrial when Joe Hill made his outburst. Obviously, Hill, not being a lawyer, did not know how to ask the judge to send the jury out of the courtroom before firing his lawyers. The anger and emotion could not have helped Joe Hill's cause with the jury.

Judge Ritchie required the lawyers to remain in the courtroom as "friends of the court." Judge Ritchie's idea was to allow Joe Hill to represent himself but have MacDougall and Scott listen to the testimony in order to make any objections that would allow Judge Ritchie to avoid error. Gibbs Smith and Foner claim that Judge Ritchie did not recognize Hill's right to defend himself and that the court erred in appointing his lawyers as standby counsel.[117]

It should come as no surprise to anyone remotely familiar with the courts that criminal defendants fire their lawyers sometimes at the most inopportune time. It is also no surprise that criminal defendants choose to act as their own attorney. Finally, in those circumstances, the trial courts with the approval of the appellate courts appoint "standby" counsel to assist and to make certain that there is no avoidable error in protecting the defendant's rights. Under those standards, Judge Richie's actions were necessary and proper.

An illustrative case is *State v. Drobel.*[118] Drobel was accused of theft. There were questions about his competency to stand trial. Nevertheless, Drobel demanded to defend himself. This demand was opposed by both the state and defense counsel on the grounds of mental incompetency. In granting the motion, the court required the defense attorneys to serve as standby counsel. The court closely questioned Drobel as to his decision, including the dangers that could be avoided by professional counsel. Drobel claimed that he was better able to defend himself because his lawyer suffered under the lack of imagination.

The Utah Supreme Court noted that the right to defend oneself in a criminal prosecution is protected under the Sixth Amendment and Article I, Section 12 of the Utah constitution. Because the exercise of this right necessarily constitutes a waiver of the important right to professional counsel, trial courts have an affirmative duty to determine that a defendant who chooses self-representation does so knowingly and intelligently. The Utah Supreme Court requires a penetrating on-the-record colloquy between defendant and the trial court to determine whether the defendant understands the risks of self-representation and accepts those risks voluntarily. Most importantly, "The defendant who conducts his or her defense incompetently with respect to standards applied to attorneys cannot assert this incompetence as error on appeal."

It is hard to imagine how Judge Ritchie could have protected the jury from the unexpected (but well-justified) outburst. After Joe Hill explained his position, it would appear that Judge Ritchie's actions were proper. If there is fault, it is the fault of MacDougall and Scott. They were the incompetent attorneys who failed to tell Joe Hill of their "strategy" and get his approval as to how to handle cross-examination. Again, when Joe Hill needed lawyers, his counsel was sadly lacking.

IV

Joe Hill and the Constitution

MacDougall and Scott failed their client by failing to understand substantive criminal law. If a lawyer intends to try a case, she should have some knowledge of substantive law.[119] None of the writers understand the extent of MacDougall and Scott's malfeasance. The Hillstrom opinion discloses a major blunder leading to questions of constitutionality in Joe Hill's trial.

When Hill was first arrested, a deputy sheriff came to him and said, "Joe, tell me where you were shot, and I'll go investigate it and get you released." MacDougall and Scott introduced that testimony before the jury. Justice Straup says in so many words, "The prosecutor couldn't have introduced that testimony. It would have been unfair." Instead of objecting to evidence of an inadmissible conversation, MacDougall and Scott introduced it themselves.

It is hard to understand what MacDougall and Scott thought they were doing by introducing the inadmissible testimony. The only rational possibility was that they were trying to bolster Joe Hill's credibility as a man with integrity who would never tell where he was shot. This interpretation is probable, because in closing argument, MacDougall told the jury that he did not know where Joe Hill was shot and that he had begged Joe Hill to tell him but that Hill continued to refuse to disclose the circumstances. MacDougal cited this refusal as evidence of Joe Hill's integrity.

The problem raised by this inadmissible testimony and the closing argument that followed was that the prosecutor, Mr. Leatherwood, commented on the story. Leatherwood argued that Joe Hill did not respond to the deputy because Joe Hill knew he could not tell a story that could be verified.

Stavis, Foner, and Smith find fault in this trial through their claim that the prosecutor commented on Joe Hill's failure to take the witness stand and testify. They are led to this error because of an incomplete reading of Justice Straup's opinion. What Elmer Leatherwood recited was the story that MacDougall and Scott introduced (i.e., that the deputy asked him to tell him what happened and that Joe Hill refused). Leatherwood's argument was in rebuttal of the claim made by MacDougall that Joe Hill's silence showed integrity. Rather, Leatherwood argued that the refusal to tell the deputy where he was shot was evidence of guilt.

Leatherwood's referral to the deputy's testimony may be an indirect comment on Joe Hill's failure to take the stand, but it's only indirect. One of the things that most people do not realize is that in 1908, the US Supreme

Court held that comment on the defendant's failure to take the stand was not improper. The Fifth Amendment privilege against self-incrimination did not apply to state court prosecutions.[120] In lay terms, this means that there was nothing legally wrong with Leatherwood commenting on Joe Hill's failure to take the stand. In fact, this holding was reiterated in a 1948 Supreme Court case.[121]

It was not until 1964, in a Justice Brennan opinion, that the Court decided that a comment on the failure to take the stand was unconstitutional in a state prosecution.[122] After deciding it was improper to comment on the failure to take the stand, the Supreme Court spent the next thirty years trying to delineate the instances in which the prosecutor's comment was material to the jury's decision. The Court looked at the strength of the evidence against the accused to see if they believed the prosecutor's comment material.[123] Further, in 1988, the Court specifically approved a comment by the prosecutor on the defendant's failure to take the stand when it "was a fair response to a claim made by the defendant."[124]

Foner and Gibbs Smith's argument of constitutional invalidity anticipated fifty years of legal development and did not account for nuances in the Supreme Court's rulings. To find that Leatherwood's comment violated Joe Hill's constitutional rights, the writers would have to demonstrate that Leatherwood actually commented upon Joe Hill's failure to take the stand, which, given the recitation by Justice Straup, is not sustainable. The writers would then have to demonstrate that the comment was material to the jury's verdict. This would be difficult in light of the jury's knowledge that Joe Hill had always refused to tell where he was wounded. Finally, they would have to demonstrate that Leatherwood was not simply responding to MacDougall's argument that Hill's failure to testify demonstrated Joe Hill's integrity.

V

Inference upon Inference

At the close of every jury trial, the judge instructs the jury as to the law. Each side has the opportunity to submit proposed instructions as to the proper law to give the jury. The court holds a "jury instruction conference" where both lawyers argue whether and how the court should instruct on a particular issue. After the judge decides how to instruct the jury, both lawyers have the opportunity to place any objections as to the instructions in the official court record. Probably the most common cause for reversal of the trial judge is improper jury instructions. The proper jury instruction is a matter of law and the Utah Supreme Court will and has overruled a trial judge if he misstates the law.

There are complaints about the jury instructions in the Joe Hill literature. Stavis, Foner, and Smith are not lawyers. They talk about a fantastic notion that the jury should have been instructed not to build inference upon inference upon inference. As Justice Straup says, "Who was building inference upon inference?" Justice Straup thought that the inference that Joe Hill was the culprit was logically connected to the evidence of the unexplained wound.

The complaints in the literature argue that the jury instructions did not reflect the law on circumstantial evidence. Here is the instruction that was given by Judge Ritchie. I call your attention to the part that says, "The facts have to be inconsistent with any other reasonable conclusion."

> You are instructed that circumstances of suspicion, if they amount to no more than suspicion, are not sufficient proof of guilt. In order to convict the defendant upon circumstantial evidence, it is necessary, not only that all the circumstances concur to show that he committed the crime charged, but that they are inconsistent with any other reasonable conclusions. It is not sufficient that the circumstances proven coincide with, account for, or render probable merely that he is guilty, but they must exclude beyond a reasonable doubt every other conclusion but that of the guilt of the defendant.

That is not the language that a court might use today, but the question is, does it misstate the law? Is it unfair to Joe Hill?[125] The instruction tells the jury that all of the circumstances not only concur in the conclusion of guilt but are inconsistent with any other result. The evidence must exclude every other consideration.

What is equally important to textual analysis is that most of the language in that jury instruction was requested by MacDougall and Scott. A party cannot complain about language requested by their attorneys. It would not be fair to Judge Ritchie to submit language and then complain that it inaccurately stated the law. Again, if this was error, it lies directly at the feet of MacDougall and Scott.

VI

You Can't Get a Fair Trial in Utah

After the close of the evidence, the lawyers summed up the case for the jury. At this time, the lawyers argued how the evidence supports the position of their client. Even in his closing argument, MacDougall showed inexperience and grossly bad judgment.

In the closing argument, MacDougall was very flamboyant. He argued evidence that was not presented to the jury. The Joe Hill literature emphasizes this evidence in their books. MacDougall said, "There were three other men in Salt Lake that were shot that night."[126] That "fact" is not in the newspapers of the day, nor was it introduced at trial. Even if true, it did not help MacDougall. I am virtually certain there were not three men shot in Salt Lake that night who did not have an explanation of where they were and who shot them. This argument merely reinforced the weakness of Joe Hill's alibi.

MacDougall argued other inadmissible evidence. MacDougall and Scott had an expert who wanted to testify that Joe Hill was shot with a steel bullet and that the bullets from Morrison's gun were lead. The judge excluded that testimony as unreliable. The judge said, "Well, the expert didn't see Joe Hill until six months after the fact. He wasn't a medical doctor, and he never made a distinction between lead and steel bullet wounds before the Joe Hill trial." The argument was improper and could have been struck by request of Leatherwood.

That was not the worst. MacDougall also attacked the integrity of the Utah court system with Joseph Smith Kimball, who had been in the constitutional convention, sitting in the jury box. He said, "Working people can't get a fair trial in Utah, and the presumption of innocence doesn't mean anything."

In closing argument, the prosecutor goes first. The defendant argues, and the prosecutor gets rebuttal. Elmer Leatherwood was a good lawyer. He had a devastating argument rebutting MacDougal's attack on the Utah state court system. Leatherwood said the court was fair and that he expected the jury to give Hill the benefit of the presumption of innocence. Leatherwood said that a Utah jury was fully capable of understanding the evidence and coming to the proper conclusion, which was that Joe Hill was guilty.

Of course, MacDougall and Scott were not allowed to say anything more about the fairness of the trial. After the damage done throughout the proceedings, it is doubtful that there would be anything left to say that would not have harmed Joe Hill's case further.

VI

Loyalty to Their Client

Lawyers owe a duty of fidelity and loyalty to their clients. That duty is not relieved by discharge by the client. This duty means that the discharged lawyers will neither say nor do anything that harms their client. The lawyer must keep his clients' confidences under all circumstances. MacDougall and Scott violated this duty and undermined Joe Hill's positions upon appeal and in the commutation hearing.

MacDougall openly challenged Hill's sanity. In the *Duchesne County Newspapers,* it was reported, "Mr. MacDougall is strongly of the opinion that Hillstrom was mentally unbalanced."[127] If he truly believed this to be the case, he utterly failed to represent his client and present a case where Joe Hill was not guilty by reason of mental instability. In fact, MacDougall told the Salt Lake City press that there would be no compromise verdicts. MacDougall asked Judge Ritchie to instruct the jury that the only acceptable verdicts were guilty of first-degree murder or acquittal.

Frank Scott was also guilty of revealing his clients' secrets. Scott attempted to save his own reputation by accusing Joe Hill of changing his mind about testifying at trial. Scott published an article in the *Telegram*.[128] Scott defended the handling of the trial. He said that Joe Hill refused to testify on his own behalf at the last minute. "The record was rotten in a different sense from what Hillstrom meant. Instead, from the beginning, he insisted that he was going to the witness chair and testify."

Scott stated that he spoke with Joseph Kimball. Kimball supposedly told Scott that until Joe Hill fired his lawyers, the jury was inclined to believe him innocent. Scott claims that Kimball told him that it was the firing of the lawyers that had the "mark of guilt."

Incredibly, Scott believed that but for the outburst (which he blamed upon a "prison lawyer"), Joe Hill would have gone on the stand and "cleared up the matter of his wounding." Scott had no doubt but that Joe Hill had additional information he could give the commutation board and thus save his life.

Scott's article is curious because it is clear that neither Scott nor MacDougall ever heard a story consistent with innocence about the gunshot wound. If they had heard such a story, MacDougall was deliberately misrepresenting the facts to the jury. MacDougall told the jury that Joe Hill had never given him any evidence about where he was wounded.

If anyone was inclined to believe Scott as to Joe Hill testifying, that person would have to assume that MacDougall and Scott were even more grossly negligent. They would have allowed their client to testify as to how he was shot without having any idea of what Joe Hill was going to say. They would have allowed the testimony without any evidentiary backup to substantiate the story.

The simple conclusion is that Scott was a liar when he said that Joe Hill would testify. In any event, if Joe Hill told MacDougall and Scott that he would testify that information should have been a closely guarded attorney client secret. Instead, Scott gave ammunition to the commutation board, which was demanding further information about the wound. Scott made it appear that Joe Hill was simply being obstinate in failing to provide further evidence.

VII

How Bad Does a Trial Have to Be?

Since writing the above, I have discovered a case that tempers my views as to whether the Utah Supreme Court should have granted Joe Hill a new trial. The question is if MacDougall and Scott were so grossly negligent that the prosecutor's case was not contradicted.

The Michigan Court of Appeals decided such a case in *Michigan v. Gioglio.*[129] This was a sex abuse case. Defense counsel presented no opening statement. Defense counsel failed to cross-examine most of the prosecution witnesses. Those witnesses who were cross-examined were not asked meaningful questions. The defense lawyer said that as a matter of practice, she never questioned sexual abuse victims. There was significant evidence that the defendant was mentally challenged. The lawyer failed to introduce or discuss that evidence. The lawyer rested the case without calling witnesses.

In summation, the defense lawyer told the jury that if they believed the prosecution's witnesses, they should convict. Upon conviction, the defense lawyer gave the prosecutor a "thumb's up" and said something to the effect that "we got him." The prosecutor was so taken aback at these actions that she wrote the court and expressed concerns over how the trial had been handled.

The defendant moved for a new trial based upon the ineffective assistance of his trial counsel. The judge found that the defense lawyer's handling was ineffective but refused to grant a new trial because the defendant could point to no new evidence that would change the result.

In a plurality opinion, the court of appeals reversed the decision. The court relied upon the Supreme Court case of *United States v. Cronic.*[130] There the Supreme Court recognized that a defendant received a proper trial under the Sixth Amendment only when defense counsel subjects the prosecutor's case to "meaningful adversarial testing."

The court of appeals concluded, "Defendant may very well be guilty and might deserve a lengthy prison term, but our constitutions do not reserve the right to the effective assistance of counsel to only those defendants who are actually innocent; rather the integrity of our criminal justice system demands that every defendant receive effective assistance of counsel."

In sum, there are defense counsel performances that are so defective that the defendant received no assistance of counsel. Had this been the standard in 1915, it is hard to know what the Utah court would have decided if this defense was raised. It is true that Justice Straup went to extraordinary lengths in both opinions to avoid criticism of MacDougall and Scott's performance. This was especially true given that there was no constitutional right to counsel at the time. Given the errors of MacDougall and Scott, the question needs to be raised.

VII

How Bad Was This Trial?

This trial was bungled by novice lawyers from beginning to end. Not surprisingly, Joe Hill was convicted by the jury. The trial was truly a litany of error. There is no way to escape the conclusion that Joe Hill's trial was in the words of his future lawyer Orin Hilton "legal but not fair."[131]

Chapter 9

The Entrance of Judge Hilton

The great act of faith is when a man decides that he is not God.

Justice Oliver Wendell Holmes

I

An Unknown Lawyer

After conviction, Hill filed a notice of appeal to the Utah Supreme Court. The labor union hired a new lawyer. MacDougal and Scott were discarded and played no part in future events. The IWW acting through the Joe Hill defense committee had now raised money. The person they hired was a famous lawyer at the time. I have to introduce you to Judge Orin Hilton, because he was the most important labor lawyer of the era. His body of labor work far exceeds Clarence Darrow's.

Hilton was born in Massachusetts and educated at Bates College, and he moved to Michigan. He served two terms as circuit court judge. He was known thereafter as Judge Hilton. He moved to Colorado around 1890. He became general counsel for the Western Federation of Miners. He did some rather spectacular trials. He got Vincent St. John off of two murder charges.[132]

Hilton was very successful at labor work. He did the spectacular trial of Steve Adams in Colorado that ended the Telluride labor wars. He was involved in the murder trials arising out of the Massachusetts textile strikes. He was involved in murder trials in Michigan and Minnesota representing labor leaders. He had a tremendous history of being very active and very successful. He was very creative and a master of courtroom procedure.

Hilton alone among the labor lawyers was not ideologically sympathetic with his clients. Hilton was an Episcopalian and a Colorado Republican at a time in which that party was conservative. Hilton always worked for money. In fact, when discharged by the IWW leadership in a dispute about his handling of a murder trial in Minnesota, Hilton waited years for his payment. He was ultimately paid by Elizabeth Gurley Flynn.

On the other hand, Hilton was very protective of his clients. He followed Vincent St. John throughout the west resolving problems. When Vincent St. John was wounded in the labor dispute in Goldfield, Nevada, Hilton was quickly there to run interference. Hilton retained the confidence of Elizabeth Gurley Flynn and St. John long after they were out of the union.

I must tell you about the most creative thing Hilton did in his labor career. In December 1905, the governor of Idaho, Frank Steunenberg, was blown up by a bomb on his front gate. Rather easily, the authorities picked up a suspect named Harry Orchard. That was the name Orchard was going by at that particular time. He also was Canadian and incidentally a bigamist. Orchard promptly confessed to the murder, but he said, "I was hired to kill Governor Steunenberg [who had been involved in labor troubles in Coeur d'Alene, Idaho] by the leadership of the Western Federation of Miners." Harry Orchard also voluntarily confessed to killing a large number of men for the Western Federation of Miners. Some of these men were beyond doubt still alive.[133]

The authorities in Idaho sent an extraordinary writ of extradition to Colorado. They kidnapped the mining union leadership on Friday afternoon when all the federal courts in Colorado were closed. The authorities put Bill Haywood, George Pettibone, and Charles Moyer on a train that was sealed. They did not send the train through Salt Lake because they knew the federal courts were open in Salt Lake. Instead they sent the train through Wyoming. The mining leadership was taken to Boise for trial.

Pettibone and Moyer actually had a case in the US Supreme Court where they challenged their extradition.[134] Justice Harlan wrote the opinion. He said, "It doesn't matter how you got there, you're there now."

Idaho tried Bill Haywood first, as the state thought they had the strongest case against Haywood. The trial of Haywood is very famous. Clarence Darrow did it. There are many books written about that trial. Orchard was the star witness, of course. Orchard testified at length as to his instructions to murder the governor from Haywood and the other leaders.

The most important prosecutor was William Borah, who had recently been elected to the United States Senate. Darrow called the defendant, Haywood, as a witness. Senator Borah cross-examined Haywood for several hours. Clarence Darrow had a two-day closing argument. Senator Borah gave the rebuttal argument, which by all accounts was extremely effective. Borah was so proud of his effort that he printed his speech and published it for the nation. Clarence Darrow prevailed, although Darrow himself expressed his belief that the most likely result to be a hung jury where the jurors could not agree on a guilty verdict.[135]

The state of Idaho had spent half of its annual budget paying the Pinkerton agents and the prosecution lawyers, and the state authorities (most particularly Governor Gooding) weren't about to see the money wasted. After Haywood's acquittal, the state set the trial of George Pettibone. Pettibone really wasn't in the leadership of the Western Federation of Miners, although he was very friendly to it. He supposedly was the originator of the explosives.[136] According to popular lore, he created something called the "Pettibone dope," which was supposed to be very explosive. Clarence Darrow started the trial but then got a massive ear infection. The Western Federation of Miners called for Judge Hilton to step in and finish the defense.

Hilton arrived the day that the prosecution rested, and what happened from there was pure genius. Hilton sat up all night reading the transcript. He calculated that no jury was going to convict Pettibone on the strength of the testimony of Harry Orchard. He guessed that Clarence Darrow was probably right in his opinion that Senator Borah had extraordinary control of Idaho juries. Judge Hilton did not want Borah cross-examining George Pettibone. Judge Hilton did not want Senator Borah arguing the case to an Idaho jury. Clarence Darrow was scared of Senator Borah after Borah closed the Haywood trial, and Judge Hilton agreed with Darrow's assessment.[137]

So Hilton came to court the next day and the judge said, "Mr. Hilton, what's your defense?"

"We aren't putting one on."

"Okay. It's time to argue."

The prosecutor objected to immediate argument. "We've got to have time to prepare."

"I'll give you to two hours." So the regular prosecutor argued his case of Pettibone's guilt. "Mr. Hilton, are you going to argue?"

"We aren't going to argue, Your Honor."[138]

Because Judge Hilton did not argue the defense case, there was no case to rebut. Senator Borah was left sitting on the sideline fuming, because he was ready to give his rebuttal argument. Hilton, by his tactics, didn't let Borah cross-examine Pettibone, and he didn't let Borah argue. The jury went out, and Hilton was right. The jury wouldn't convict on the testimony of Harry Orchard. The historian Page Smith noted that conventional tactics are conventional largely because they work. It is the measure of genius to deliberately stray from conventional tactics when called for by a particular situation. By any measure, Hilton's abandonment of conventional trial tactics was genius.

Hilton had prior contact with Salt Lake City. In 1905, non-Mormons in the American Party took over the government of Salt Lake City. They put in a new police force, which unfortunately was corrupt. In 1906, the police force ran a crooked poker game. They brought in an expert crook to run the game. Ultimately, Police Chief Sheets was charged with defrauding Alexander McWarter of $10,000. This was a significant sum in 1907.

The con man, a Mr. Parrent, got scared and went to Colorado. He hired Hilton. Hilton decided that the only way he could get Parrent off was to plead him guilty. This sordid affair is absent from standard Utah history texts. There was a trial of the police chief. A lawyer named Soren Christensen got the chief out of his jam on a technicality. The prosecutor had charged the chief on a racketeering statute. Soren Christensen discovered that all of the offenses were misdemeanors and would not support a felony charge.[139] Soren Christensen would later figure prominently in the Joe Hill matter and the aftermath.[140]

II
Crime According to Judge Hilton

Hilton's contemporary, Clarence Darrow, was a philosopher and the companion of the literary giants of the day. Reading Darrow is a trip into Nihilism. In his book, *Crime: Its Cause and Treatment*, Darrow argued that there is no such thing as crime other than actions of which society at any particular moment disapproves. There are no criminals, only individuals who did things of which society disapproves. Darrow was always able to go on the lecture circuit and draw a crowd. Darrow was a showman. He did legal cases for the notoriety. There was no good reason for the atheist Darrow to get involved in the publicity stunt of evolution in Tennessee. He handled the Scopes trial merely to entertain his liberal friends (and become immortalized in four feature films entitled *Inherit the Wind*).

Judge Hilton was not in Darrow's class as an intellectual gadfly. He knew his classics well enough to go into the silent movie business as a screen writer of Roman and Greek literature.[141] He is never mentioned by Menken or others in the national press. Today, Darrow is known as much for his knowledge of psychology and philosophy as he is for his trial prowess. (Darrow could pick juries and give long closing arguments, but he was not particularly good at trial procedure and evidence. He would often farm the details of a trial out to subordinate lawyers.) Hilton, on the other hand was a master of everything in the courtroom.

Hilton left only one piece of speculative literature. In August 1906, he wrote a piece for the Masonic magazine *Sons of Colorado*. Entitled *Crime and Criminals*, the article is a thorough exploration of Judge Hilton's mind. Hilton first distinguished between individuals of good families who occasionally cross the line of criminality and children who come from criminal families. Hilton believed, "Criminals begat children endowed with criminal propensities or at least with decided tendencies towards crime as were sufficient to demoralize their parents." The home life of criminals further confirms the likelihood of continued familial crime. "In brief, the more criminal their parents are (*sic*) the more crime will flourish, and the more crime flourishes the more criminal parents there will be found to begat vice and propagate criminals."

Hilton believed that a child caught in such a trap would develop a moral nature so distorted that crime would appear to him to be virtue. "He may and in a certain sense does appreciate the difference between right and wrong, but his almost total lack of shame, ambition and conscience, leads him to class as good that which panders to his perverted tastes ..." Hilton found remorse totally lacking or that remorse is only that one is caught in his criminality.

Hilton noted the propensity of professional criminals to work for days observing their victims before striking. "The true, habitual criminal would rather steal a dollar than to honestly earn ten with one half the time and labor." Hilton was a true believer in Social Darwinism. Criminals belong to a degenerating class—cunning, drunken, charming, and idle.

Hilton approved of penal reforms but believed them only effective if the separate classes of criminals are segregated. Hilton did not believe that penal reforms by themselves would check the criminal class. "Something must be done to check the development of born criminals and to prevent normal youth from becoming incorrigible."

Hilton advocated taking "born criminals" from their parents. Criminality should be attacked in the cradle before the young criminal has opportunity to propagate more criminals. Crime is a disease and should be treated as such by isolating the born criminal from society. Prison sentences should be indeterminate so that the criminal will be isolated as long as he has propensity to offend.

Hilton believed in phrenology, a pseudoscience based primarily on the measurements of the head. "The experienced and skillful detective becomes so familiar with different forms and types of criminals that he can frequently identify one upon sight." Among the physical characteristics of criminals are the pointed or sugar loaf form of head or a low, flat-topped skull, which indicates the family comes from a degenerating family. Foreheads that recede are indicative of criminality and "a low order of intelligence." Persons with prominent lower jaw are prone to crimes of violence. Hilton had a number of other "rules," including the lack of beard, which indicates criminal intent.

While Hilton's view of humanity in general is rather gloomy, it is important to note that he thought he could discern criminality by physical form. He obviously believed that Vincent St. John did not exhibit the head shape of a murderer. Further, he also believed that Joe Hill's phrenology would not support a charge of violence or murder.

Phrenology was neither a creature of the ancient past, nor was it unique to Judge Hilton. Numerous Mormon leaders believed in it and had their head shape examined by believers in the science. Hilton seems odd compared to the Darrow, who was up on the latest Freudian theory. Hilton thought that he was scientific, but it was a science not recognized today.

III

A Freemason in Utah

Judge Hilton was a Freemason. At the turn of the twentieth century, this would not have been unusual for a middle-class white American male. The end of the Victorian era saw a flourishing of ritualistic lodge-based fraternal organizations. Justice Straup was an Odd Fellow and a Knight of Pythas. Frank B. Scott was a Moose. There were also organizations such as the Elks, Woodsmen, and Rotary. Shortly thereafter, a white male could join either the Kiwanis Club or the Ku Klux Klan. A black male could join the Prince Hall Masonic Order. A Catholic could become a Knight of Columbus.

Masonry in Mormon Utah has a great deal of religious, political, and economic baggage. Simply put, Mormons were not interested in standard Masonry, and the Masons excluded Mormons from their lodges. The reasons for this mutual antagonism, which lasted until 1984, are both historical and found in doctrine.[142]

Masonic literature clearly spells out their position as a nonsecular, nonpolitical movement. Indeed, religion and politics are not to be discussed within the lodge. The nonsecular position of Masonry did not apply in Utah. Masonic ritual and the definition of a Masonic Supreme Being are historical reasons for the great divide between Mormonism and Freemasonry.

Explanation for the doctrinal divide requires consideration of early Mormon history. After their expulsion from Missouri, the Latter-day Saints settled in Nauvoo, Illinois. This was a time of great theological growth. The theological innovations of the Nauvoo period included polygamy, but polygamy must be understood within the concept of the family of man and man's relationship to God. Although not directly mentioning polygamy, the culmination of Joseph Smith's exposition of the nature of God as a perfected man and the nature of man as a God in embryo was found in his *King Follette Discourse* given shortly before his death. In support of his doctrine of the family of man and God, Joseph introduced what is now known as the Temple Endowment Ceremony.[143, 144]

Nauvoo was also a hive of great Masonic interest among the Mormons. Many prominent Mormons, including Brigham Young and Hyrum Smith, had been members of the lodge prior to the organization of the Church. In Nauvoo, the members formed a number of lodges, and indeed one of the prominent buildings in Nauvoo was the Masonic Lodge Hall. Joseph himself joined and was quickly passed through the initial degrees of Masonry. At the same time, there always was a hint of irregularity among the non-Mormon Masons about the Mormon lodges.

In developing the Temple Ceremony and in latter Mormon theology, there is facial borrowing from Masonic ritual and symbols. There are Masonic symbols on the exterior of the Salt Lake Temple. When the Utah Saints established ZCMI (Zion's Cooperative Mercantile Establishment), their cooperative store, the entrance to the establishment was under the Masonic "all-seeing eye." This being said, any casual reader of Masonic literature and the Mormon Scripture Pearl of Great Price easily understands that the founding "myths" of Masons and Mormons have nothing in common.[145] Nevertheless, from the Nauvoo period on, Masons have viewed Mormons as having corrupted the principles of Masonry. The antagonism on the part of the Mormons is undoubtedly influenced by the great number of Masonic brothers in the mob who murdered Joseph and Hyrum Smith.

After the epic migration to the Great Basin, Mormon leadership showed inconsistent but mostly scant interest in restarting Masonry. It is true that in the most famous portrait of Brigham Young, he wears a Masonic pin. There was some talk of obtaining a dispensation from a European source, but it went nowhere. My suspicion is that the simple necessity of effort in settling the west, together with the renewed emphasis on the Temple ceremony, left little time for extracurricular activities.

As non-Mormons begin filtering into Utah, they brought Freemasonry. From the beginning, it was a distinctly non-Mormon enterprise.[146] For many years, Masons justified exclusion of Mormons on the grounds that by supporting polygamy, Mormons were law breakers, thus violating Masonic principles. They also objected to allowing the Nauvoo-period Masons visiting privileges in their lodges with the explanation that Nauvoo Masonry was "irregular."

Michael Hunter observed that by the turn of the twentieth century, the Nauvoo Mormon Masons had died. The ban on Mormon membership continued and needed further doctrinal explanation for the violation of one of the most basic rules of Masonry. Utah Masons had to explain why a non-sectarian society banned a religious sect. That explanation was made in 1921 by a grandmaster of the Utah Lodge and a Congregationalist minister Samuel H. Goodwin in his tract *Mormonism and Masonry.*

Goodwin explained the exclusion in terms that the Reed Smoot protestors could understand. The issue was church doctrine. In particular, Goodwin questioned the Mormon concept of plurality of gods. The Mormons well understood the challenge. It was the same argument that freedom of religion meant that one could be free to accept a religion as long as it was a mainline protestant sect.

Of course, underlying Goodwin's arguments was the fact that Utah Masons, like all Utah non-Mormons, resented the Saints' electoral power and economic exclusionary policies. Although the absolute percentage of Mormon membership in Utah was lower around the turn of the twentieth century than it had been previously and would be in the future, a determined Mormon political effort would always be decisive. This fact was much resented.

It was important that Judge Hilton was a member of a group that both excluded Mormons and was actively hostile to them and their beliefs. This group hostility came to no good in handling the Joe Hill case. Hilton came into Salt Lake City prejudiced and knowing full well who he was going to blame for the conviction. His prejudice would lead to positions that otherwise would not make sense to the reasonable advocate.

IV

A Mormon Masonic Fraud

Individual Mormons were not innocent in this debate. In 1924, the Eighth Circuit Court of Appeals (the federal court immediately below the Supreme Court) upheld the convictions of Dominic Bergera and Mathew Thompson for mail fraud.[147] Thompson was a Mormon. He had set up a rival Masonic Order, which he called the "American Masonic Federation." Thompson claimed a dispensation from a small and disintegrating Scottish Lodge. This fact was, of course, not disclosed to the men who purchase advanced degrees from the defendants. It appears that this Masonic organization existed only in the minds of the defendants. All of them knew that their claimed authority was spurious.[148]

The defendants essentially set up a Masonic Diploma Mill whereby they solicited monies for advanced Masonic degrees throughout the nation, representing them to be authentic.

"Such a degree, with so many designations of supposed Masonic distinction and greatness, must have been among the best sellers on the Masonic market conducted by the defendants." The defendants knew that their claim to authenticity was false and fraudulent. "[T]hat it had no temples or buildings or lodge halls of any kind; that it seemed to consist of Thompson's dwelling quarters and the printing press engaged in the constant work of turning out diplomas and degrees." Nor were Thompson's associates innocent of the true nature of this fraud. "The jury could well believe that his (one of the defendants) trip to Europe and his conduct upon his return in carrying on with the organization as in the past, were a part of the plan to further advance the work in which the defendants were engaged of alluring innocent victims and profiting financially thereby."

Members of recognized Masonic bodies were outraged by this blatant fraud on the craft. Once again, it appeared that Mormons were not only stealing from their secrets and organization but were also illegitimately turning a fraudulent profit.

The peak of Thompson's enterprise was after 1911 and was centered in Salt Lake City. Given the emphasis Masons place upon "regularity," there could not have been a worse offense. Again, a regular Mason such as Judge Hilton could not fail to be enraged by this fraud easily blamed on the Mormons. This antipathy came to no good in the Joe Hill case.

Chapter 10

The Arrogance of Judge Hilton

Lawyers spend a great deal of time shoveling smoke.

Justice Oliver Wendell Holmes

I
Bad Habits

Judge Hilton had bad habits for a trial lawyer. The modern rules of professional conduct limit the ability to try a case in the newspapers. Rule 3.6 precludes extrajudicial statements to the media, particularly in criminal trials. Lawyers are precluded from giving opinions as to the guilt or innocence of the accused.

Judge Hilton was not so restrained. For example, in 1907, Hilton represented Vincent St. John in a murder trial based upon an alleged conspiracy. The trial judge had received a threatening letter. Judge Hilton made the "Sensational Charge" that the letter was "written and dispatched with sole purpose to influence the jury against the defendant." Hilton charged that the letter was sent by one of the prosecution witnesses in an attempt to frame St. John.[149] Hilton followed that accusation with another sensational press release alleging that the Nevada mine owners schemed with Senator George S. Nixon and Colorado mine owners to frame the allegation against St. John.[150]

In addition to his habit of providing good copy to the press, Hilton made a score of enemies in courtrooms around the west. In the Steve Adams trial, Hilton repeatedly mocked and insulted the prosecutor.

These habits did not advance Joe Hill's case. Appealing to the national press merely stoked Utah regionalism. Hilton vilified everyone who had any responsibility in the Joe Hill matter. In other matters, Hilton would pick a personality to vilify. In Joe Hill's case, Hilton was particularly antagonistic to Chief Justice Straup, repeatedly attacking the Chief Justice for fairness and insulting his intellect. Before Joe Hill was executed, Hilton had made enemies of virtually the entire Utah community. He also provoked a revival of the anti-Mormon crusade at a time when feelings were beginning to heal.

We cannot tell Hilton's motives. Certainly, Hilton was playing the double game of legal representation and propaganda. It appears that Judge Hilton was a publicity hound and could not restrain his instincts. Whatever the reason, Joe Hill's case became an international cause, and Judge Hilton was in the middle of the controversy with his snide tongue and biting sarcasm. By the end of the case, the legal merits were subordinated to propaganda, and it is clear that at least Joe Hill was more interested in his legacy than his life. It is also clear that Judge Hilton, wittingly or unwittingly, became a propaganda tool for the IWW.

II

Hilton's First Appeal

Hilton was a brilliant trial attorney, but never before and never after did he handle any appellate matter. We know this because we can search *Westlaw*. The only time Hilton ever showed up as counsel in an appeal was as the representative of Joe Hill, so he took on a legal matter where he had no experience.

Appellate law differs from trial law in that the advocate is expected to be more cerebral. He is expected to know case precedents and statutes. An appeal is presented by brief and oral argument. Oral argument is not the appeal to passion found in a trial closing argument. It is not an argument over the "facts" developed in the trial court. It is an argument, first and foremost, about the application of the law by the trial judge. Hilton struggled with those standards. He wanted to give and gave the justices an appeal that asked the court to find the jury verdict unreasonable.

The Utah press was not kind to Judge Hilton's argument. They quoted his opening characterization of the trial as "outrageous and unheard of." Although Hilton was speaking directly about the discharge of MacDougall and Scott, his comments set the tenor of the argument as seen by the press. The press reported that his main argument was one of mistaken identity. The press merely reported that the state's attorney general argued that the state's evidence was a complete chain of evidence that Joe Hill was the assailant. The state attorney's argument must have been subdued, as the reporter gives him only one paragraph.[151]

Hilton's first argument considered by the court concerned the applicability of a recent Utah Supreme Court case. Hilton told the court that Joe Hill's case was like another case, incidentally, known as *State vs. Hill*. Coincidentally, the case was known as *State vs. J. Hill*, and I was worried that the "J" stood for Joseph. The court doesn't tell us the first name of the defendant, sparing history further confusion.[152]

In this other *State vs. Hill* case, the sheriff of Midvale and four men called "Austrians" were drinking in a saloon. The "Austrians" didn't speak English. They were probably from Yugoslavia, Croatia, or Serbia. Two robbers came in and started shooting. They killed the sheriff. One of the "Austrians" had a gun. He got off a shot and wounded one of the assailants. Before the wounded criminal died, he refused to tell the name of his confederate.

The authorities arrested this Hill defendant. Like our Joe Hill, this J. Hill was a manual laborer. Convinced they had arrested the right culprit, the authorities took the case to trial. "J. Hill" was convicted of the murder of the sheriff. But when the Utah Supreme Court looked at the matter, the justices found, "The witnesses said that the robber was over six feet, this guy's five foot nine." The witnesses said the robber was brown-eyed. This guy's blue-eyed. The witnesses said that the robber had a dark complexion. This guy's got a light complexion. The robber had a good sized nose while this defendant has a thick or chubby nose. We don't think that this J. Hill is the robber, and we're going to remand for a new trial." In the new trial, "J. Hill" was acquitted.

Hilton argued that Joe Hill's case was analogous to the "J. Hill" case. In Joe Hill's case, the authorities did not have definite eyewitnesses. Without definite eyewitnesses, Hilton argued, it is the same lack of proof. The court said, "No. It's not." The distinction was that Joe Hill had been wounded and that there was a witness who placed a man of his description in the vicinity of the crime. The wound was evidence that tied our Joe Hill to the crime. Further, Joe Hill told an alibi that the jury was free to disregard. Thus, the Utah Supreme Court rejected Hilton's main legal argument.

Hilton then argued the credibility of the prosecution witnesses. He said that it was impossible for the witnesses to see or identify Joe Hill. The Utah Supreme Court said that the jury was the sole decision maker when it comes to credibility. As an appellate court, they felt bound by the credibility decisions of the jury as to evidence supporting the jury's decision. Simply put, the Utah Supreme Court was not going to decide which witnesses were believable and which were not. Every lawyer who has done appellate work knows that arguing credibility will not persuade the appellate court and is perhaps the greatest error to be made.

I have one quote. I thought this expressed the concept appropriately. This is Judge Alex Kozinski of the Ninth Circuit speaking at BYU Law Review. He says, "When a lawyer resorts to a jury argument on appeal, you can see the judges all sit back and give a big sigh of relief. We understand that you have to say all these things to keep your client happy, but we also understand that you know and that we know and you know that we know, that your case doesn't amount to a hill of beans."

The credibility argument greatly impressed Stavis, Foner, and Gibbs Smith because they were writing their histories on the actual philosophical guilt or innocence of Joe Hill. They felt the Utah Supreme Court was not only unfair but in actuality wrong because the court did not evaluate the quantity and quality of the trial witnesses. It is clear that Judge Hilton did not "muster the evidence" or tell the court what evidence supported the verdict and why it was insufficient. Hilton merely argued that the jury was wrong. This argument has been rejected every time it has been made.

Stavis and Foner cite possible arguments, demonstrating facts they perceived to have had relevance. Many of those facts (three other men shot in Salt Lake City) were not introduced in trial or were not supported by evidence admitted at the trial (lead versus steel bullet). Barrie Stavis argued that it was reversible error when Judge Ritchie refused to allow the introduction of hearsay evidence indicating that Morrison was scared of particular men. These rulings on the admissibility of evidence were within Judge Ritchie's discretion.

None of these arguments were raised by Hilton on appeal. The Utah Supreme Court obviously could not rule on the legal decisions of Judge Ritchie if Judge Hilton did not raise the evidentiary matters in his argument. The court had no independent mandate to investigate every possible error that history might discover at some time in the future.

It is important to remember that Joe Hill refused to testify, and therefore no facts came from him. It should not be surprising that the Utah Supreme Court's facts did not align themselves with Joe Hill's version of the story as told to his supporters and the press. Dr. Foner, in particular, goes into detail as to why he thought Justice Straup misjudged the credibility of the witnesses. Justice Straup, on the other hand, was simply reciting the evidence that supported the verdict. This is what the Utah Supreme Court would have done in any other case. It does not mean, as Foner suggests, that the decision of the Utah Supreme Court was fixed or that the justices were biased against Joe Hill. It means the court performed the same review of alleged errors of law as in any other case. It means that the court refused to go beyond its constitutional mandate to decide questions of law and not questions of fact.

Hilton also argued that the conviction was based solely on circumstantial evidence and should be overturned on those grounds. Justice Straup said, "It's really not all circumstantial evidence. In fact, there is fairly direct evidence." The direct evidence included the wound, the alibi, and the general description of a man fitting Hill's appearance in the area. Justice Straup cited other cases in which conviction was based solely upon circumstantial evidence. Convictions before and since have been based upon much less evidence than the evidence introduced against Joe Hill. It is simply not correct to say that there could be no conviction without direct eyewitness testimony. Joe Hill is not the only murderer whose conviction was upheld with some circumstantial evidence. In fact, there have been murder convictions upheld on only circumstantial evidence.[153]

It is important for the lay reader to understand that the Utah Supreme Court did not decide the ultimate issue of guilt or innocence. They refused to make that decision. It was not their job, as it has never been the job of any appellate court. The justices simply decided that there were no wrongfully decided legal questions and that the jury had a reasonable basis for finding Joe Hill guilty. Dr. Foner particularly was in error in castigating the Utah Supreme Court for not appreciating the "true" facts of the case and reversing the jury. Reading the court's opinion demonstrates that Justice Straup explained in great detail the reasons why the court had no responsibility or even ability to overrule a properly supported jury verdict.

Based upon their view of Hilton's arguments, the Utah Supreme Court upheld Joe Hill's conviction. At the time, the Joe Hill supporters were greatly shocked by the decision. In the cold light of history, there is nothing unusual about the court's refusal to involve itself with a case that concerned disputed questions of fact. In today's jurisprudence, the same result would have been reached. There is nothing new or shocking about the court's opinion. There was no reason to expect any other result given the arguments made to the court.[154]

Elizabeth Gurley Flynn and other Joe Hill supporters were shocked that Judge Hilton could lose a case.[155] Judge Hilton was shocked because the Utah Supreme Court did not agree with his oratory. He had swayed juries for years. He was not accustomed to being found wrong on the law. Again we find arrogance by Hilton. He expected everyone in Utah to immediately recognize his brilliance and act accordingly. When it did not happen, he reacted badly. In doing so, he helped neither his client nor himself.

III

I don't have to tell where I was shot

Joe Hill, with the assistance of Hilton, filed a petition to the Utah Commutation Board.[156] In those days, the commutation board consisted of the three justices of the Utah Supreme Court, the attorney general, and the governor of the state. The attorney general previously argued the appeal. The three justices, of course, ruled on the appeal. The Utah Commutation Board was not the appellate court. It only had the power to reduce or eliminate a criminal sentence. It did not have the power to grant a new trial. The validity of the conviction was established.

The only new factor in the commutation proceeding was the governor, William Spry. William Spry was a Republican but also a Mormon. He was from Toole County. His major administrative experience was as president of the Latter-day Saint Southern Mission. His only experience with labor difficulties was an attempt to mediate the 1912 Bingham Canyon copper strike. He was not particularly successful in that attempt. His biography was commissioned by the family and written by Leonard Arrington. The title is *Man of Firmness.* I do not think he was firm about anything. He was the only member of the board who did not have a college education. He was intimidated by the non-Mormon educated lawyers. Further, Spry exercised no independent political skills to override the formal legalism of the lawyers.

At the commutation board, Joe Hill no longer had a Fifth Amendment privilege against self-incrimination.[157] Joe Hill had been convicted. His conviction had been upheld. If Hilton and Joe Hill wanted the board to rule in Hill's favor, Joe Hill had to tell the board where and when he was shot. The justices were adamant about Joe Hill providing evidence that would explain his actions on the night of the murders and how he was shot. Hill and Hilton refused to give any further information unless and until the board granted Joe Hill a new trial. The Utah Commutation Board did not have the authority to grant a new trial but could have reduced Joe Hill's punishment to imprisonment. Obviously, Hilton thought he could do better in a new trial than MacDougall and Scott. In asserting a right to a new trial, Hilton refused to acknowledge the duty to provide new evidence to the board. Even Governor Spry got the point. Governor Spry said to Hilton, "Can't you make this man talk?" Hilton and Hill continued to say, "We have the presumption of innocence. The state has to prove I'm guilty, and the fact that I got wounded is irrelevant." The non-Mormon lawyers on the board insisted that the protection against self-incrimination no longer applied and Hill must give new information.

It is clear that Hilton, by this time, was more interested in propaganda than Hill's life. The night before the commutation hearing, Hilton was reported as saying, "We are going to argue the case on the records of the trial. While I was not connected with the trial in the district court, yet I hoped the Supreme Court would grant a new trial. When we appear before the pardon board, there will not be any new evidence brought before it, and I still presume that Hillstrom will refuse to give the story of his wounding on the night of the Morrison murders ... It will be based upon the record in the case and especially those portions of the testimony on which was based the circumstantial evidence on which he was convicted."[158]

On the day of the hearing, Hilton reiterated that he was not going to present new evidence but that he was going to reargue the circumstantial evidence upon which Hill was convicted. "Hilton intends to cite a number of cases where convictions were had on circumstantial evidence and which were later reversed by the courts when the real culprit was taken into custody or confessed."

That Hilton was dealing not in law but propaganda is explained. "Hillstrom is a peculiar man. He seems to me to be a man who wants to be a martyr for a cause. I believe he will go to his death rather than give the name of the woman in whose company he claims to have been with when he was shot ... I do not think the Supreme Court of Utah put the law right when it decided the Hillstrom case, especially the part of the decision which relates to the defendant refusing to take the stand in his own behalf."[159]

Hilton was not considering how his arguments were playing in the general Utah press and among the general Utah population. The day after his argument, the *Salt Lake City Herald* published a rebuttal. It should be considered in its entirety:

Judge O. N. Hilton of Denver is sufficiently a lawyer to know that the sort of venom he spilled upon Salt Lake yesterday by medium of an afternoon newspaper contravenes his obligations both as a citizen and as a member of the bar. Apparently he is not sufficiently a lawyer to know that it is not within the province of the board of pardons to grant a new trial to a condemned man, nor sufficiently a lawyer to caution his client against appearing before that body with nothing more than protestations of innocence. ...

When Joseph Hillstrom's irascible Denver attorney denounces the board of pardons for refusing his client a new trial, he appeals to prejudice because he knows that interference with the courts is not legally possible to the pardon board. When he talks of the methods of execution in Utah, he but arraigns a whole state for decreeing the death penalty for murder. When he raves of the severity of law enforcement in Utah, he coaxes an amused smile from a community and a state long prone to believe that maudlin mercy is interfering with the process of justice. When he declares that he 'can only say Hillstrom's complaint has always been earnest and consistent that he was deprived of a fair trial,' he goes beyond the lawyer's traditional privilege of resorting to the nearest tavern and cussing the board; he arraigns himself with the hotheaded corner loafer whose vituperation is in inverse ratio to the knowledge of the situation.[160]

But Hilton was not willing to stop. "This result is only an example of the iniquitous system of having a pardoning board consisting of five members all but one prejudged the cause and solemnly announced the accused was guilty." He called the Hillstrom matter the most unjust, wicked travesty of justice that has occurred in the west. Hilton said that he could easily demonstrate Joe Hill's innocence to an impartial board without argument. He attacked the men who would constitute the firing squad as judicial murderers. Joe Hill would die true to the principles of "free speech and free thought as exemplified by a free trial."[161]

The justices were not buying the argument that Joe Hill still had the presumption of innocence and that the circumstances of his wound were irrelevant and protected by Joe Hill's right to not incriminate himself.

Hilton then became obnoxious. He lectured the board on the inequity of executing a person on circumstantial evidence. In fact, the justices were not likely to listen to his argument on circumstantial facts because Hilton had written a treatise on evidence where Hilton took the opposite view. In the commutation opinion, the court essentially quoted Hilton's book.

There were actually three hearings before the commutation board. At each hearing, Hill and Hilton refused to provide any new information unless and until Joe Hill was granted a new trial. Hilton started a letter-writing campaign. In the *Utah Electronic Archives*, there are thousands of petitions to the board and Governor Spry. There are at least five or six thousand letters written to the board, none of which were on point to the rather legalistic minds of the justices. The justices wanted to know if there was "any other new evidence." The petitioners merely complained that the trial was unfair. Helen Keller wrote a letter. President Wilson weighed in against the execution. The Swedish ambassador became involved. Once again, Joe Hill refused to give even the ambassador any new evidence.[162] The protestors were putting pressure on Governor Spry and the board to do something except shoot Joe Hill. On the other hand, Spry and the board were receiving pressure from Utah sources to be tough on crime by shooting Joe Hill.[163]

Hilton published an offer by Elizabeth Gurley Flynn of $500 for any new information. No new information was forthcoming.[164]

Unfortunately, the board took a rather formal legalistic view in response to Joe Hill and Judge Hilton's refusal to meet their demand for new evidence. The board had four lawyers. They were all Big Ten educated, all non-Mormons. All depended upon Mormon votes to stay in office. All were scared that if they looked soft on crime, they were going to lose the Mormon vote. Joe Hill would not give them new evidence to work with in fashioning a remedy that would meet the objections of all parties.

The attorney general and the justices did not want to shoot Joe Hill. They certainly did not wish to create a labor martyr. The desire to find a political solution goes so far that two of the justices said to Hilton and Joe Hill, "Take the sheriff. Go out in confidence. Find the people. If you can make your story believable, we'll let you go." Joe Hill and Hilton replied, "No. We aren't going to do that, the burden of proof is on the state. I have the presumption of innocence. I don't have to tell anything. The fact I got wounded is irrelevant."

The problem was the lack of political will by board to resolve the matter given the intransigency of Judge Hilton and Joe Hill. With the board's tin ear to national political realities, it could not find some justification to commute the death sentence and put Joe Hill in jail. If the board with its non-Mormon lawyer majority had found a political solution, we wouldn't be talking about Joe Hill today. No one would have cared. The board and particularly Governor Spry could have politically worked their way out of the protests and the Joe Hill problem. They chose not to do so. They denied commutation, relying upon the excuse that they were expected to be tough on crime and that Hilton, Hill, and the protestors had not shown that there was any new evidence justifying any other result.

Hilton started a publicity campaign. He was in all the newspapers. He challenged the justices to a public debate on the merits of the case. All through downtown Salt Lake, Hilton placed big posters proclaiming Joe Hill's innocence and the injustice of his impending execution.[165] He told the newspapers that Joe Hill's pending execution was an event equivalent to the Mountain Meadows Massacre.[166] It was the worst thing that ever happened in the west. It was the biggest farce. Hilton offered to establish a law school in Salt Lake and admit the justices to the kindergarten class. In response, the commutation board issued a statement to the press:

> [T]he complete record of the case illustrates that Hillstrom was given a fair and impartial trial.

> The defendant and his counsel ... have offered no evidence that refutes that evidence which placed the guilt of the Morrison murder upon Hillstrom and which was sufficiently conclusive for the jury to find him guilty.

[N]ot one scintilla of new evidence was shown that might exonerate him, although every opportunity was afforded Hillstrom and his counsel.[167]

In his refusal to even entertain the thought of arguing new evidence justifying a pardon, Hilton played the propaganda game. It is clear that Joe Hill knew the game and was playing along. Execution meant immortality, and that was more important than attempting to provide new evidence.

If Hill and Hilton had wanted commutation, they would have had to exhibit a much more humble attitude before the board. Rather than humbly try to explain the circumstances, they arrogantly challenged the authority of the board. It is not hard to foresee the outcome of this campaign.

IV

Judge Hilton's Speech

Joe Hill was executed on the nineteenth of November 1915. Hill told Hilton, "I don't want to be buried in Utah. Get my body out of Utah." The IWW took the body to Chicago, where the union held a public funeral. Twenty thousand people attended. The principal orator was Judge Hilton. Judge Hilton not only spoke, but he also had a stenographer there to take down his words. Hilton had his speech published and distributed throughout the country.

This is the tenor of Hilton's words. "The genesis of this transaction and this tragedy out of Salt Lake City, took its rise in the bureaucratic power of the Mormon Church. Bureaucracy denominated by greed, selfishness, and a plenitude of power that has defied the government of the United States and today teaches its followers that supreme power resides in the church, and that it will visit with vengeance upon any questioning of its power. Don't let anybody, my friends, fool you into the belief that the lying story that this power is diminishing. It was never so powerful, as it is today, never before so dangerous."

He talked about Mountain Meadows. He called the church "the vilest thing in our national life today, that hideous, slimy monster, which has made this crime (Hill's execution) here, possible." He claimed that a Mormon jury convicted him and a Mormon governor refused commutation.

"Do you believe, men and women of Chicago, that this silent form would be in your midst today, if Joe Hillstrom had been a good Mormon, paying his tithe promptly to the church, had two, three, or four wives to call him 'husband'? I do not say this was done by direct influence other than, the imponderable and undefined, but always present and always dominating fear of the Mormon Church. While they have some very wise and just laws in their statute books, when you test them by their real day, every day application is guided and governed entirely by what Mormon leaders may decree as to the expediency of the moment."

At that point, Judge Hilton published his book nationally. He went on a nationwide speaking tour. At every stop he reiterated that the Utah Supreme Court was corrupt and that the Church was calling the shots. It was the Church that wanted Hill dead.

It did not take long for Utah to react. An example of Utah reaction was found in the *Park City Record*. "After looking at the picture of O. N. Hilton, the Denver Attorney, in last Sunday's Herald, one can easily imagine that he is an IWW, or anything else that savors of viciousness and hate. His looks alone should debar him from practice in the courts of Utah—to say nothing of his slanderous attack on the supreme court of Utah and the vile epithets hurled at the state officials in his funeral oration of the murderer, Hillstrom, in Chicago recently. The question which annoys the good people of Utah is: 'Why the unnecessary delay on the part of the bar association against Hilton. Is it possible that certain members of that brainy body are afraid?'"[168]

V

War on the Mormons

No Mormon could fail to understand Hilton's words. It was not the copper bosses who shot Joe Hill. It was the Mormons. Hilton, the Mason, was resurrecting all of the bitterness of the Reed Smoot hearing. He was accusing the Mormons of using their numbers and power to crush labor.

He was using the unpopularity of the Mormon Church to bolster the union claim of being a portion of mainstream America. Accommodation with the Church was impossible. Once again the Mormons would have to defend their rights to exist as a religion under the First Amendment. Once again the argument was made that the First Amendment only protected established protestant churches and that Mormons did not come within that group.

Hilton's words were a declaration of war by the union against the Church. In the Mormons' eyes, that declaration was followed by numerous threats on the life of Governor Spry. Those threats were interpreted as directed at Mormonism and its followers. While the Church did not directly respond, other portions of the Utah community took up the challenge and the battle.

Chapter 11

Soren Christensen's Bad Day

Carve every word before you let it fall.

Justice Oliver Wendell Holmes

I
Punishment of   Judge Hilton.

It was not only the Mormons who understood Judge Hilton's words. No one in the Utah legal community could miss the importance of Hilton's challenge to the court's impartiality. Rather than an attack only upon the Church, it was an attack upon the lawyers, the court, and their character. Hilton claimed that the court was run by the Church for the benefit of the Church. Hilton said that it was the Church that wanted Joe Hill shot. He claimed that the justices were mere puppets, taking orders from Church President Joseph F. Smith. This was a challenge that the court system could not ignore.

The controversy can be followed in the pages of the Salt Lake press, most particularly the *Salt Lake Telegram*. The statements of Judge Hilton had a statewide impact. Together with the threats on the life of Governor Spry, Hilton's speech inflamed the state against the IWW in particular and unionism in general.

Less than a month after the Joe Hill funeral, the *Telegram* gave the first indication of the coming war. It noted that the grievance committee of the Utah Bar was meeting with the "ultimate object" of the disbarments of Attorney O. N. Hilton "on account of certain of his activities and utterances in the case of Joseph Hillstrom." The paper reported that Hilton had been under investigation even prior to Joe Hill's execution but that the bar felt it prudent to wait until after the ending of the case.[169]

On December 1, 1915, Governor Spry weighed in on the controversy. "Men of Hilton's stamp—any lawyer who would prevaricate as much as he has done—should have no standing at a Utah bar . . ." Governor Spry had received a copy of the stenographic report of Hilton's funeral oration. "Personally, there is no doubt in my mind as to what should be done with Hilton. The bar should purge itself of all such attorneys." The paper noted that the disbarment of Hilton would be sought on the grounds that he maliciously attacked the Utah Supreme Court at his Chicago speech.[170]

Two days later, on December 3, 1915, the bar began to act. Bar President Herbert A. Macmillan referred the matter to the grievance committee. "Rule 23 of the rules and regulations for practice before the supreme court of Utah, which has been in effect since 1896 and which rule will figure in the disbarment proceedings, provides that any member of the bar guilty of improper or contemptuous conduct concerning the court, either in or out of court, will be treated as in contempt of court."

The bar saw the implications of Hilton's anti-Mormon screed. They quoted him, "No doubt the authorities could ultimately carry out their threats. Knowing the power of the Mormon Church in Utah as I do, I presume they can deprive me of my right to practice." This statement was presumed by the bar to be misconduct because Hilton again claimed the Utah Supreme Court was subject to the power of the church.[171]

The bar moved quickly. On December 21, 1915, charges were filed against Judge Hilton. "The proceedings and accusations are based principally upon a speech made by Hilton at the Hillstrom funeral in Chicago where the attorney attacked the governor, members of the Supreme Court, attorney general, jurors who tried Hillstrom and the Mormon Church."

The disbarment proceedings were a multi-religion and multi-party effort. The bar was represented by Charles Varion, a Republican non-Mormon who had come to Utah to prosecute polygamy. He stayed on after the Church abandoned the practice. He was the leading light of the Utah Constitutional Convention and very much beloved by both Mormons and non-Mormons. The other lawyer was Frank Nebecker, a Mormon Democrat from Logan.[172]

The three specific charges against Hilton were that he attributed the origin and administration of state laws to the Mormon Church; he failed to maintain the respect due the courts of the state; and he tried to procure a new trial for Joe Hill when not possible under the law. Most importantly, in doing so, he resorted to "falsehood, exaggeration and concealment of the truth."[173]

Judge Hilton was never a person to take accusations lightly. He filed an answer with the Utah Supreme Court. He denied all wrongdoing. He denied that he intended to cast contempt or ridicule upon the several justices of the court and denied that he brought the laws or administration of justice in Utah into disrepute or contempt. His main defense was that the Chicago speech was beyond the jurisdiction of the court. He further argued that anything he said was protected by the provisions of the First Amendment. The answering brief was signed by attorney Soren X. Christensen.[174]

Even with the conciliatory the tone of his brief, Judge Hilton soon destroyed any indication that he wanted peace with the Utah Supreme Court. "I shall not take back anything said while in Salt Lake or any other place."[175]

Judge Hilton decided that he had other pressing business precluding him from attending the session of court deciding his disbarment. Justice Straup was particularly upset at Hilton's absence. Hilton left the matter in the hands of Soren X. Christensen and Ira Snyder of Denver. Snyder argued that there was nothing in the speech warranting disbarment. Snyder was forced to admit that it would be reprehensible if the attorney told the audience untruths. Christensen argued that even untruths would not be sufficient to disbar Hilton. Justice Straup took issue with Christensen, saying that Hilton had deliberately misstated what the court had written. Snyder and Christensen argued that the First Amendment protected Hilton's speech.

Christensen was forced to admit that the members of the Utah Supreme Court, the attorney general, the trial judge, and several members of the jury were not members of the Mormon Church. The prosecuting attorney, Nebeker, asked if there was any evidence of influence or interest in the Hillstrom case by the Mormon Church. Christensen was forced to admit, "I never heard of such thing. Hilton had no right to make such statements as he did without acquainting himself with the facts."

Attorney Snyder informed the court that Hilton was surprised and aggrieved by the court, thinking that he attempted to impeach the honesty or integrity of the courts of Utah. Justice Straup did not accept that argument. "If the motives and the intentions of the respondent are to be taken into consideration why is he not here to offer his statement?"[176]

A lawyer cannot without specific evidence accuse the court of wrongdoing.[177] There are First Amendment cases discussing a lawyer's right to criticize a court's decisions. Law review articles are written dissecting the words and reasoning of appellate courts. Hilton did not tell the Chicago crowd that the Utah Supreme Court reviewed the trial court record only for error. Instead, Hilton told the funeral gathering that the court got marching orders from the Church. A lawyer cannot make up accusations against a court without evidence supporting his beliefs. Hilton was merely speaking out of his anti-Mormon Masonic prejudice. As Soren Christensen was forced to admit, Hilton spoke without knowing the facts. Hilton went over the line under any circumstance. The court system simply cannot function if an attorney (an officer of the court) makes up falsehoods.

It is fortunate for Judge Hilton that he had friends who would represent him under the circumstances. The justices were furious, and they had intended to release that fury on the head of Judge Hilton. Deprived of their target, they aimed their anger at Soren Christensen.

Soren Christensen had a bad day before the Utah Supreme Court. Anyone who has argued an appeal has to feel very sorry for that poor man who had to stand before the court and take the righteous abuse directed at Judge Hilton.

Soren Christensen was probably not a bad choice to try to meet the justices' anger. Christensen's parents were Mormon converts who settled in the Scandinavian settlements in Sanpete County. Christensen was never baptized a member. He attended Brigham Young University under the school's founder, Karl G. Maeser. He read law in the office of the future Senator King. He returned to Sanpete County to start his practice but moved to Salt Lake City, where he specialized in criminal law. After the Joe Hill trial, he felt isolated in Salt Lake City and moved his family to San Francisco, where he purchased a hotel. As a member of the California bar, Christensen handled many criminal and domestic cases in the appellate courts successfully.[178]

Even sending the well-respected Soren Christensen had no effect upon the court. Justice Straup wrote a blistering opinion, complete with literary language that only Judge Hilton could understand. Hilton had made a specific target of Justice Straup. Hilton had mocked and insulted the Chief Justice by name. Hilton had called Justice Straup stupid and corrupt. The only form of retaliation available to Justice Straup was his opinion, and in that opinion, Justice Straup told the world how little he thought of Judge Hilton and his tactics.

The year after Utah disbarred Judge Hilton, his alma mater, Bates College, awarded his an honorary LLD for his long service to the profession. In 1924, when Justice Straup took a hiatus from the court, a very humble Judge Hilton requested reinstatement. He said that he was sorry for his language. The Utah Supreme Court reinstated him.

II
Can a Lawyer Abuse the Court?

Since writing the above, there has been a case delineating a lawyer's constitutional First Amendment right to verbally abuse the court system. In *Kentucky v. Berry,*[179] a lawyer was disciplined after intemperate remarks toward a legislative ethics committee. The bar association brought disciplinary charges based upon Rule 8.2's prohibition of a lawyer's statements relating to the impartiality of a tribunal.

Berry sued in federal district court, alleging that the rule impinged upon his First Amendment freedom of speech. The district court rejected this challenge. Restrictions on a lawyer's speech have repeatedly withstood constitutional challenge "on the grounds that states have a compelling interest in maintaining public confidence in the judiciary." By prohibiting reckless statements as to the qualifications and integrity of a judicial officer, the rule decreases the likelihood that false statements will occur. The rule merely requires a lawyer to speak with greater care and civility than a non-lawyer citizen. "Scurrilous" language is prohibited under the rule because "such language promotes disregard for the law and the judicial system."

Therefore, it appears that Justice Straup was correct in his opinion that Judge Hilton's attribution of Mormon influence to the Utah court decisions was subject to discipline.

Joe Hill Conspiracies.

We should be eternally vigilant against attempts to check the expression of ideas which we loathe.

Justice Oliver Wendell Holmes

I
Did the Mormons Kill Joe Hill?

As I prepared this book, I thought of different methods of analysis that explain the Joe Hill result. I have come to believe that turn of the twentieth century Utah was a hive of conspiracy theories. Those theories often conflict and often explain the viewpoints of the participants. Mormons were convinced of an anti-Mormon conspiracy. The Masons and other non-Mormons were equally convinced of Mormon conspiracies to control the state. The IWW members were paranoid about management and with good reason. The mine owners and other non-Mormon businessmen were equally convinced of an anarchist plot to destroy capital.

Utah is not unusual with respect to conspiracy theory at the turn of the twentieth century. Even the progressive hero Theodore Roosevelt indulged in conspiracy theories. When accepting the "Bull Moose" nomination, Roosevelt told his followers that "they stood at Armageddon."

Mormon paranoia is easily explained. Professor Paul Johnson of the University of Utah reasoned that Mormons were the only religion that fought the militia of two states and the United States Army. The long polygamy wars had forged an identity not only as a religious group but also as a people.

This identity leads to a simplistic worldview in which people are divided into Mormons and non-Mormons. This view continues today. I have met very few Mormons who can tell the difference between a fundamentalist Christian and a Pentecostal. Few can tell the difference between a mainline Protestant church and an evangelical church. I have unsuccessfully told Mormons about anti-Catholic violence.

In Joe Hill's case, the only Mormons directly involved were jury members and Governor Spry. As I have shown, attacks on the fairness of Utah by the petitioners for clemency were taken as attacks on Mormonism. Church members particularly resented the attacks and threats upon the life of Governor Spry. In that regard, Mormon conspiracy theory came into play. When Judge Hilton attacked the Church and the Mormon people, they certainly knew the rules of engagement and reacted accordingly.

The Utah non-Mormon paranoia is equally understandable. The Mormons had a disconcerting habit of voting as a block. The hierarchal nature of church leadership led to suspicion of ulterior motives, and it was most certainly true that the Mormons' actions were motivated by views that were frustratingly different. There is no better example of this paranoia that the Salt Lake City Ministerial Alliance. Those gentlemen were willing to dispute anything and everything on principle.

In Joe Hill's case, the non-Mormon officials were aware that they held office with the support of the Church. As I have shown, the popular Utah press was an effective counterweight to the thousands of letters pouring in to Utah in support of Joe Hill. That, of course, had to be taken into account.

Given the outcome of the two major strikes, labor had a right to be paranoid about industrial mining conditions in Utah. Neither strike succeeded. On the other hand, I have shown that prejudice against the IWW presence in Utah was not as significant as suggested. Their one strike at Tucker elicited two articles in the Carbon County press and slight notice in Salt Lake. The one instance of violence against the IWW was the Salt Lake City riot. The aggression was two sided and definitely escalated by the union members. There was no free speech movement in Salt Lake, and the officials did not harass the members. The reaction of Chief of Police

Grant to IWW members coming through the city was measured and fair. It cannot be forgotten that this invasion of the city by IWW workers occurred while Joe Hill was in jail and awaiting trial.

Likewise, management of the national mining enterprises was convinced of the conspiracy of labor. The court decisions and constant harassment of labor demonstrate this paranoia.

In evaluating conspiracy theories about this trial, I have found that the simplest explanation has the greatest possibility of truth. The major theme of this book has been that the sheer incompetent actions of Ernest D. MacDougall and Frank B. Scott, combined with the arrogance and prejudice of Judge Hilton, constituted good and sufficient causes of the conviction and execution of Joe Hill.

The reason that a simple explanation is best is that a conspiracy to kill Joe Hill would be hard to concoct and harder still to hide. A conspiracy to Joe Hill would require the complicity of multiple members. A conspiracy to frame and kill Joe Hill could not have been concocted by two or three people in a closet. For example, conspiracy does not explain the presence of Joseph Kimball on the jury. If the Mormon leadership wanted Kimball on the jury, they would have had to include Judge Ritchie in the conspiracy. Elmer Leatherwood would have had to be complacent in the plan. Most importantly, MacDougall and Scott would have had to be in on the scheme as well because they had the absolute power to dismiss Kimball. If the scheme was hatched by the "copper bosses," it becomes even more attenuated.

It would be extremely hard to concoct an anti-labor conspiracy in Mormon Utah with Utah's multiple prejudices. Axel Steele, the union baiter, was a Presbyterian. That denomination was not favorable to the Latter-day Saints. Salt Lake's pastor was a signatory to the Reed Smoot protest. For years, the Presbyterians ran a mission to the Mormons in Salt Lake City in the charge of Sheldon Jackson.

II

Conspiracy of the Authors

I have been critical of Dr. Foner and Barrie Stavis (but not Gibbs Smith) largely because I believe they fell into conspiracy theory. Believing Hill innocent, they looked elsewhere for explanations and found conspiracy where none exists. In *Conspiracy: How the Paranoid Style Flourishes and Where it Comes From,* Daniel Pipes explains that documentation and scholarly attributes are not always indications of a non-conspiratorial mind.

> When the topic is conspiracy, it is often difficult to distinguish truth from falsehood. In part, this is because objective criteria—logic and evidence—do not clearly demarcate on from the other. Further muddying the waters, individuals in the know sometimes make untruthful claims, serious scholars endorse wild claims and pseudoscholars pass off their work as genuine research.

The value of this work on Joe Hill or any work is not the number of footnotes but the convincing power of the argument. Having the advantage of a life in court, I have experienced similar questions and outcomes for more than thirty years. I have rarely encountered a true conspiracy.

The only claim for superiority I make is that of the trial lawyer. I claim to know what I don't know. I claim a healthy skepticism about the affairs of my fellowmen. I have learned to reject the simple explanations put for complicated affairs. Life is messy. Unless one has the true belief and ideological confidence found most often in conspiracy theories, the rational mind must deal with this unpleasantness.

Most of all, I reject the notion that either history or law has the power of ultimate knowledge. I am very cynical of people who know that which cannot be known.

After I did a run through of the oral presentation in my office, I went in and talked to one of the young lawyers. He said, "Well, was he guilty?"

I said, "I'm not God." If you think history can resolve this matter, you're probably a graduate student looking at a ceiling for a bullet that's been gone for fifty years. If you've ever tried cases in the law courts, you have a little bit of humility about the ability of the law to decide ultimate questions of guilt or innocence. There was one time in Fairbanks I had a hard-fought case in front of a judge who had been my friend before going on the federal bench. He's now on the Ninth Circuit, and his name is Andrew Kleinfeld. After two and a half weeks of fighting and fighting, I lost. I came in to the bar luncheon. I was pretty despondent. Andy, Judge Kleinfeld, looked at me and said, "Have you ever considered that the jury might have been right?" So, I'm rather agnostic about actual guilt or innocence, but I do say, as I said before, this was one of the worst pieces of lawyering of all time. That is where the evidence takes the argument.

Postscript

The riders in the race do not stop short when they reach the goal. There is a little finishing canter before coming to a standstill. There is time to hear the kind voice of friends and to say to one's self: "The work is done." But just as one says that, the answer comes: "The race is over, but the work never is done while the power to work remains."

Justice Oliver Wendell Holmes

There is always something else to be stated with respect to Joe Hill. I realize that my position that trial law has not changed over the past century gives rise to presentism. It would be equally easy to find that the resistance to unions in Utah and among the Mormons was the result of the Joe Hill matter.

I am not convinced that that is the case. While Mormons might not join labor unions, they are perfectly happy in the equally paternalistic Fortune 500 corporations or the military. In my time in Alaska, numerous Mormons were labor union members. They belonged to all of the major unions, including the Teamsters. In Alaska, the Teamsters actively recruited members from almost any occupation and were thus the modern equivalent of the "One Industrial Union Grand."

Further, I am not convinced that union members are not good Mormons. I did my church mission in Michigan and Ohio. There were numerous good union members who became good Mormons.

There is always the example of my wife. As a schoolteacher, she always supported the National Education Association. She has her reasons for doing so. She believes that the NEA protects their membership from arbitrary dismissal by the greater community.

In some respects, I believe the Joe Hill case to have significance to the labor movement, independent of its relationship to Mormons. Today's Mormons do not even know about Joe Hill. I reject a conflict between today's Mormonism and trade unions. By rejecting this conflict, hopefully I have moved on from the ideological conflicts raging in early twentieth-century Utah.

Salt Lake City
2011

Endnotes

Chapter 1

1   http://www.youtube.com/watch?v=yr6SMAJQW8Y

2   There is significant controversy about plagiarism by Dr. Foner. A graduate student, James O. Morris, accused Foner of lifting much of the text from Morris's unpublished master's thesis. I cite Dr. Foner not for the quality of his research or his academic integrity but for the ideology he represents.

3   Sugar House Park is the former location of the Utah Penitentiary where Joe Hill was executed. It is now a public park.

4   Ball, David and Keenan, Don, *Reptile,* Balloon Press, New York, 2009.

5   I use the word "myth" in the historical and not the pejorative sense.

6   *In re Hilton, 158 Pacific 691* (Utah 1916)

7   *State v. Hillstrom,* 150 Pacific 935 (Utah 1915).

8   *In re Hilton,* 158 Pacific 691 (Utah 1916).

9   The authorities only charged Hill with Morrison's murder with the intent that if he were acquitted, they would have the ability to try him again for the murder of the Morrison son.

10   Wallace Stegner presumed the other robber to be a Swedish acquaintance of Hill named Otto Appelquist. Appelquist disappeared from Salt Lake City after the crime and was never thereafter found. In the absence of positive evidence, I am not willing to speculate.

11   *State v. Clopten,* 2009 UT 84.

12 "Justice Daniel N. Straup," *Utah Bar Journal,*
Spring–Winter 1986. Chief Justice Daniel N. Straup.
Born 1862 Millersburg Pa. Graduate Valparaiso
University 1883. Admitted to the Indiana Bar 1888.
Board of Directors of the Salt Lake City Unitarian
Church; *History of the Bar and Bench of Utah,* Interstate
Press Association, Salt Lake City, 1913.

13 "Strike at Tucker," *Price (Utah) Carbon County News,*
1913-06-12; "Conflicting Reports" *Carbon County
News* 1913-06-19; "End of Strike," *Salt Lake City
Herald,* 1913-06-14.

14 "Railroad Agents Warn Trespassers away from Tucker,"
Salt Lake City Herald, 1913-06-12.

15 Axel H. Steel or Steele. He was born in 1865 in
Sweden. He emigrated to the United States in 1880.
He was a deputy sheriff in Salt Lake County in the
1910 census. Steele was Presbyterian at a time when
that denomination seriously confronted the Latter-day
Saints. "Funeral Service for Axel Steele set for Thursday,"
Salt Lake Telegram, 1919-10-27. He died Salt Lake City
1919 of cancer. Steele would have been forty-eight when
the IWW riot occurred.

16 There is much evidence of Steele doing actual police
work. He appears to have been the deputy who was sent
out of state to either deliver or return prisoners for trial.
The limited involvement in strike breaking is referenced
in "Deputy Steele has record of long service in strikes,"
Salt Lake City Herald, 1913-08-13.

17 "Dispute over American flag is cause of Downtown
Riot; Four are shot: IWW Held as Gunman," *Salt Lake
Herald,* 1913-08-13; "IWW Chiefs in County Jail,"
Salt Lake City Herald, 1913-08-14. Steele apparently
was a hothead. He was referred to as a "gunman."
"Meeting threat," *Eastern Utah Advocate (Price, Utah),*
1913-08-15.

18 "Salt Lake City Scene of Riot," *Carbon County News,*
1913-08-14; "Brief Legal Items," *Eureka Reporter,*
1913-08-22; *Manti Messenger,* 1913-08-15

19 "Morgan says he was pulled from box and kick (*sic*) in face," *Salt Lake City Herald,* 1913-08-13.

20 "Morgan Denies Story," *Salt Lake City Herald,* 1913-09-04; "Will Renew Meetings Threat," *Herald,* 1913-08-18.

21 "Busy in Ogden," *Salt Lake City Herald,* 1913-09-21.

22 Brother of LDS apostle and future Church president, Heber J. Grant.

23 "IWW on Way to Denver Fight," *Salt Lake Telegram,* 1914-03-23.

24 The only mention of the IWW in the *Telegram* was a report from the San Pedro Police. Even then the Salt Lake press confused the issue. They reported that the missing Otto Applequist was a songwriter for the IWW. See "Asserts Murder Suspects are Street Car Bandits," *Salt Lake Telegram,* 1914-01-22.

25 "My First Murder Trial," *Salt Lake City Telegram,* 1914-06-23.

Chapter 2

26 Flynn, Elizabeth Gurley, *The Rebel Girl: My First Life 1906-1926,* International Publishers, New York, 1955.

27 This is precisely the tactic advocated by the Franklin Roosevelt first administration to spur employment in the Great Depression.

28 Camp, Helen C., *Iron in Her Soul; Elizabeth Gurley Flynn and the American Left,* Washington State University Press, 1995, p. 84.

29 Haywood, William, *Bill Haywood's Book,* International Publishers, New York, 1929, p. 280.

Chapter 3

30 Brooks, John Graham, *American Syndicalism, the IWW,* p. 15.

31 Holmes's views were only accepted in the 1920s by a school of thought known as "Legal Realism." To some

extent, they were exaggerated. Holmes did not discard precedent. He believed that in the use of precedent, the judge should undertake an examination of the policies underlying the earlier case. If those policies were persuasive, there was no need to depart from prior law. If they were not persuasive, then the court could justifiably depart.

32 *Lochner v. New York,* 198 US 45 (1905).

33 *Holden v. Hardy,* 169 US 366 (1898).

34 Herbert Spencer (1820–1903). English philosopher who popularized social Darwinism and opposed all social reform movements.

35 *Adair v. United States,* 208 US 161 (1908).

36 *Coppage v. Kansas,* 236 US 1 (1915).

37 The judges were the equivalent of the "scientific historians" of the day who denied that they had any philosophy in their judgments but were guided only by evidence. Holmes's realism not only influenced law but also the progressive historians.

38 *State v. Spies,* 122 Illinois 1 (1887).

39 Brooks, p. 15.

40 Borah, William E., *Closing Argument of W. E. Borah in Haywood Trial,* Boise, 1906.

41 Changes in ballistics testimony led future Supreme Court Justice Felix Frankfurter to conclude the trial was flawed. Frankfurter and his wife, Miriam, were prime organizers of the non-communist opposition to the execution. The antagonism between Frankfurter and Harvard president Lowell might have been a prime cause of the rejection of clemency by the governor.

42 *People v. Schoon,* 171 P. 680 (Cal. 1918).

Chapter 4

43 Arrington, Leonard, *Great Basin Kingdom,* Harvard University Press, 1958, p. 401.

44 *Paul v. Salt Lake City R. Co.,* 34 Utah 1, 95 P. 363 (Utah 1908).

45   Mr. Armstrong was secretary of the two anti-Mormon political parties (the Liberal party and the American party). He was also a Republican advocate of free silver. *See entry in Bar and Bench of Utah.*

46   *Grant v. Lawrence,* 37 Utah 450, 108 P. 931 (Utah 1910).

47   Jurors Owen and McDowell were both foreign born and not members of the LDS Church.

48   Powel, Allan Kent, "The Foreign Element and the 1903–1904 Carbon County Coal Miners' Strike," *Utah Historical Quarterly* 43 (Spring 1975), 125–54.

49   *Deseret Evening News,* January 4, 1904.

50   Peck, Gunther, "Padrones and Protest: "Old" Radicals and "New" Immigrants in Bingham, Utah 1905–1912," *Western Historical Quarterly* 24 (May 1993).

51   *Doctrine and Covenants,* Section 27.

52   Eshom, Frank, *Pioneers and Prominent Men of Utah,* Salt Lake City, 1912, p. 174; Richard H. Peterson, *Utah Historical Encyclopedia; Brigham Young University High School, http://www.byhigh.org/History/Knight/Jesse.html.*

53   Tallmadge, James E., *Articles of Faith,* Deseret Book, Salt Lake City.

54   One of the leading senators in opposition to Smoot taking his seat was the Idaho senator, Fred Dubois. Dubois, like Frank Cannon, had started his career as a Republican but soon disagreed with his party on the issue of silver. Like Cannon (a close friend with whom he traveled to the Orient), Dubois became a Democrat. Regardless of party, the primary moving factor of Dubois' political career was hatred of Mormonism. By 1908, Fred Dubois was gone from the senate. In the 1906 election, he was unable to fuse the Populists with the Democrats. The Mormon-dominated southeast turned Republican and helped elect a legislature to turn out their old enemy in favor of William E. Borah. Their vote can be explained more in terms of self-defense than in terms of party loyalty.

55 Flake, Kathleen, *The Politics of American Religious Identity: The Seating of Senator Reed Smoot, Mormon Apostle,* University of North Carolina Press, 2004.

56 Roberts, B. H., *Recent Discussion of Mormon Affairs,* "The Improvement Era" Salt Lake City, 1907. Kathleen Flake argues that Church doctrine also changed as a result of the Smoot hearings. I would argue that this is misreading of Mormon beliefs. Roberts made plain that Mormon beliefs on marriage had not changed and that the country had no right to prescribe belief. Examination of the beliefs Roberts held essential to religious Mormonism demonstrate no change. Further, if one examines the "Manifesto" issued by President Woodruff, one finds that the primary justification is the continuance of the Mormon doctrine of Temple salvation for the dead. Simply put, President Woodruff had no intention of abandoning the doctrine he considered essential, even at the cost of giving up plural marriage. For anyone who doubts the continuity of Mormon belief, I refer them to Harold Blooms's *The American Religion* and any number of websites by evangelical Christians denying that Mormons are Christians.

57 *Toneray v. Budge,* 95 P. 26 (Idaho March 1908).

58 Roberts, B. H., *Comprehensive History of the Church,* Deseret Book, 1965 edition, pages 408–12.

59 Of the industrial workers jurors, Henry McDonough and George Nichols were not members of the LDS Church.

Chapter 5

60 *Gideon v. Wainwright,* 372 US 335 (1963).
61 *Powell v. Alabama,* 287 US 45 (1932).
62 *Bute v. Illinois,* 333 US 640 (1948).
63 *Chandler v. Fretag,* 348 US 3 (1954).
64 Rules of Professional Conduct, Rule 1.1. "A lawyer shall provide competent representation to a client. Competent representation requires the legal knowledge,

skill, thoroughness and preparation reasonably necessary for the representation."

65   When confronting a Ponzi scheme, I filed the first involuntary Chapter Seven bankruptcy proceeding in the history of the state. For a colorful description of fraud on the last frontier, see *In re Bonham* in its various proceedings.

66   "Boy is Witness in Opening of Trial," Salt *Lake Telegram*, 1914-06-18.

67   This is further evidence that Dr. Foner plagiarized James Morris' paper. Mr. Morris spells his name "McDougall." Morris apparently had no more information on MacDougall than anybody else.

68   Smith also spelled the name "McDougall."

69   "My First Trial," *Salt Lake City Telegram*, 1914-06-23.

70   Conversation with Judy Pacheo, chief clerk of the Wyoming Supreme Court, December 27, 2010.

71   *Kelsey v. District Court of First Judicial District of Platte County*, 139 P. 433 (Wyoming 1914).

72   Chief Clerk of the Utah Appellate Courts.

73   MacDougall signed the roll of attorneys on June 4, 1914.

74   "Socialist Speaking," *The Kemmerer (Wyoming) Camera*, 1914-11-11.

75   "Local News," *Carbon County News*, 1915-03-19.

76   *Tinkler v. Powell*, 151 P. 1097 (Wyo. 1915).

77   "Local News," *Duchesne County (Utah) Newspapers*, 19-16-04-29.

78   My mother's family came from the Uintah Basin. I spent the summers of my early youth on my grandparents' farm in Duchesne County. I personally experienced the conservative Latter-day Saints of the basin.

79   My uncle, Merlin Perry, is from Myton.

80   "Macdougall Requested to Leave," *Duchesne County Newspapers*, 1917-10-27.

81   *History of the Bar and Bench of Utah*, Interstate Press Association, Salt Lake City, 1913.

82 *Minah Consol.Min. Co. v. Briscoe*, 89 F. 891 (9th Cir. 1898).

83 "Sunshine Coal Mine to Buy F. B. Scotts Coal Mine at Hales." *Eastern (Price) Utah Advocate*, 1907-10-10; Scott Incorporates His Hale Mine," *Eastern Utah Advocate*, 1907-10-10.

84 "Court News," *Deseret News (Salt Lake)*, 1908-12-19.

85 "Debs Addresses Large Audience," *Salt Lake Herald*, 1908-09-08.

86 "First Shot at the Middleman," *Deseret News*, 1910-01-21.

87 "Moose Lodge Conducting Big Initiation," *Eureka (Utah) Reporter*, 1922-09-15.

88 "Canadians Banquet," *Deseret News*, 1910-05-25.

89 *Cooke v. Cooke*, 248 P. 83 (Utah 1926).

90 *In the Matter of Scott*, 296 Pac. 1113 (Nev. 1931)

91 "Asked to investigate records of suspect," *Salt Lake Telegram*, 1914-01-27.

92 94 P.3d 186 (Utah 2004).

Chapter 6

93 Spence, Gerry, *Win Your Case*, St. Martin Griffin, New York, 2005, p. 85.

94 Friedman, Rick and Patrick Malone, *Rules of the Road*, Second Edition, Trial Guides, Portland, Oregon, 2010.

95 Federal Rules of Evidence, Rule 401. "'Relevant Evidence' means evidence having any tendency to make the existence of any fact that is of consequence to the determination of the action more probable or less probable than it would be without the evidence."

96 Federal Rules of Evidence, Rule 403. "Although relevant, evidence may be excluded if its probative value is substantially outweighed by the danger of unfair prejudice, confusion of the issues, or mislead the jury, or by considerations of undue delay, waste of time, or needless presentation of cumulative evidence." Exclusion

of evidence under Rule 403 is an "extraordinary remedy."
In re Davis, 246 B.R. 646 (Bk. Utah 2000).
97   "I'm Going to Mars and Organize Canal Workers for
IWW," *Salt Lake (Utah) Telegram,* 1915-09-30.

Chapter 7

98   *Gardner v. State,* 234 P.3d 1115 (Utah 2010).

99   I've long believed that the jury system does not function
particularly well in death penalty cases. This is because no
error may be allowed. I have followed closely the debates in
the Court. I think like Justice Stevens, I am no longer willing
to adjust the mechanisms of death. I am not persuaded by
the Court's reference to foreign law or evolving standards of
decency. I would abolish the death penalty simply because it
imposes too great of cost on the country. I see in Utah the
gyrations the legal system goes through when politics dictates
a capital sentence. The courts simply do not function well
when every precaution must be taken against error. There are
multiple appeals followed by habeas petitions in the federal
system. Even if the state is somehow able to maneuver through
these obstacles, we must consider the psychological toll taken
upon lawyers, jurors, and judges who must deal with a
criminal as if his rights are the most important in the world.
That, of course, does not account for the difficulties faced by
the penal institution that, if the lawyers ever succeed, must
actually put a person to death. If we speak only of finances, it
is much cheaper to put the person who really does not deserve
attention in prison for a long time. The cost to the system is
much greater.

I learned this in Alaska. My partner, Ralph Beistline,
went on the bench in time to handle a particularly
egregious murder. He sentenced four young men who
had killed a native to find what killing felt like. I asked
him if it bothered him to handle the murder. He said,
"No. I gave them ninety-nine years for the crime and
fifteen years for using a gun. I banged my gavel and
went to lunch." In Alaska, a criminal must serve five

years plus one-third of the sentence before eligibility for parole. I think those boys will have learned their lesson after spending forty-three years in prison. The system worked much better, the courts were free to deal with other problems, and good people did not lose sleep. Thus, the philosophical and legal arguments seem irrelevant to the good of society.

100 In Alaska there was a large "Free Jury" movement propagandizing the notion that the jury was free to disregard the law led by an ex-convict named Frank Turney. Turney was known to parade in front of the courthouse, bleating at prospective jurors. On occasion, he wore a halter with a hangman's noose.

101 *Clinton et al v. Englebrecht*, 80 US 434 (1871). The Mormon view of this controversy is found in future Church President Joseph Fielding Smith's *Essentials in Church History.*

102 *Elmer O. Leatherwood*, "Biographical Directory of the US Congress," 1872–1929. Graduate of University of Wisconsin law school, 1901.Admited to Utah Bar in 1901. District Attorney of Salt Lake County, 1908–1916. Republican member of Congress, 1921–1929; *History of the Bar and Bench of Utah.*

103 *History of the* Bar *and Bench of Utah.* Morris Latimer Ritchie. Born 1858. Admitted to the Bar of Kansas, 1879. Admitted to Utah Bar, 1891. Served in Kansas legislature as a Republican. Judge Ritchie was an Episcopalian.

104 "Trial of Hillstrom is Begun Today," *Salt Lake Telegram,* 1914-06-010; "Three Hillstrom Jurors Chosen," *Salt Lake Telegram,* 1914-06-11; "No new Jurors are Secured to Try Hillstrom," *Salt Lake Telegram,* 1914-06-12; "Hillstrom Jury Not Decided," *Salt Lake Telegram,* 1914-06-16; "Hillstrom Jury is Complete," *Salt Lake Telegram,* 1914-06-17.

105 In his letter to the *Telegram,* Joe Hill cited his belief that his trial was unfair because he believed that only jurors summoned to hear only his case could properly sit. At

his second sentencing, he made the same argument to Judge Ritchie.

106 Doctrine and Covenants 124:132. The Doctrine and Covenants is a compellation of revelations given to Joseph Smith and regarded by the Latter-day Saints as Scripture. The Nauvoo Stake High Council was a deliberative body second in importance only to the apostles of the Church.

107 Jensen, Andrew, *Latter-day Saint Biographical Encyclopedia,* Church of Jesus Christ of Latter-day Saints, Salt Lake.

108 Compton, Todd, *In Sacred Loneliness,* Signature Books, Salt Lake City, 2001.

109 J. Golden Kimball was a member of the Church's First Quorum of Seventy, the third-most-important deliberative body in the church. He was widely known for his colorful sermons, which often contained mild swear words.

110 Spencer Woolley Kimball, 1873–1985. President of the Church of Jesus Christ of Latter-day Saints, 1973–1985.

111 Gardner, Hamilton, "In Memoriam Joseph Kimball 1851–1936," *Sons of the American Revolution 1936;* Whitney, Orson, *Life of Heber C. Kimball* Deseret Books, Salt Lake City: Compton, Todd, *In Sacred Loneliness,* and Eshom, Frank, *Pioneers and Prominent Men of Utah,* Utah Pioneer Publishing Book Co., Salt Lake City, 1913.

112 Edger Paul Boyko, 1918–2002. Attorney General of Alaska in the Walter Hickel first administration, 1967–1968.

113 In one rural Alaska case, I used all of my preemptory challenges and seated a jury that had a majority of native Alaskans. What the opposing party did not know was that my client was part native and a member of an Alaska Native Corporation. I have never thought that brilliant cross-examination or argument had much to do with the favorable result.

Chapter 8

114 The question of actual innocence as a ground for a new trial has been considered by the United States Supreme Court. At least two members of the current court, Justices Scalia and Thomas, believe the constitution only guarantees a proper trial and that the fact the defendant might be actually innocent is irrelevant even in death penalty cases.

115 I am indebted to my brother, Colonel Douglas A. Lougee, MD, MPH. Colonel Lougee is command surgeon for the United States Southern Command. He has responsibility for all United States military medical operations in the Caribbean and Latin America. As such he is a recognized expert in third-world medicine.

116 Rules of Professional Conduct, Rule 1.2.

117 Judge Hilton's statements to the Utah press reflected his expressed view that the failure to declare a mistrial upon Joe Hill's outburst was the primary error in the trial. That was not how the appeal was presented or argued before the Utah Supreme Court.

118 *State v. Drobel,* 815 P.2d 724 (Utah App. 1991).

119 Rules of Professional Conduct, Rule 1.1 requires that a lawyer be competent.

120 *Twining v. New Jersey,* 211 US 78.

121 *Adamson v. California,* 332 US 46.

122 *Malloy v. Hogan,* 378 US 1 (1964).

123 *See US v. Hastings,* 461 US 499 (1983).

124 *US v. Robinson,* 485 US 25 (1988).

125 *State v. Hansen,* 734 P.2d 421 (Utah 1986). "It is the duty of the judge to instruct the jury on relevant law. Accordingly, the judge may, over the objection of the defendant's counsel, give any instruction that is in proper form, states the law correctly, and does not prejudice the defendant."

126 "Accuses State of Framing Story," *Salt Lake Telegram,* 1914-06-26.

127 "Local News," *Duchesne County Newspapers,* 1915-10-02.

128 "Hillstrom could have saved self, says his lawyer," *Salt Lake Telegram,* 1915-08-24.

129 *Michigan v. Gioglio,* 2011 WL 173182 (Mich. App. April 5, 2011).

130 *United States v. Cronic,* 466 US 648 (1984).

131 Amazingly, MacDougall and Scott made Joe Hill's situation worse after their discharge. Scott published an article in the local press. He claimed that Joe Hill had agreed to take the stand and that the only reason for the conviction was Hill's later refusal to testify. MacDougall responded to this publication by accusing Scott of violating Joe Hill's confidences.

Chapter 9

132 *1921 Bates Alumnus.* By 1921, Hilton had moved to San Francisco. He went into the silent movie production business. His obituary is in the February 1933 *Bates Alumnus.* Interestingly, Bates College gave him an honorary LLD in 1917 after he had been disbarred by Utah.

133 Martin, MaryJoy, *The Corpse on Boomerang Road,* Western Reflections Publishing Company, Montrose, Co., 2004.

134 *Pettibone v. Nichols,* 203 US 192 (1906).

135 Lukas, J. Anthony, *Big Trouble,* Simon and Schuster, New York, 1997.

136 "Bomb that killed Gov. Steunenberg manufactured in Denver," *Deseret News,* 1906-03-01.

137 Borah, William E., *Haywood Trial: Closing Argument of W.E. Borah,* Bancroft Library, University of California.

138 "State Rests in Pettibone Case," *Salt Lake Herald,* 1907-12-25; "Pettibone Trial May Stop," *Salt Lake Herald,* 1907-12-31; "Defense Ready for the Jury," *Salt Lake Herald,* 1908-01-01; "Pettibone Case in Jury's Hands," *Salt Lake Herald,* 1908-01-04.

139 "Parrent is Identified," *Salt Lake Herald,* 1907-02-22; "Crook is Pitted Against Lawyer," *Salt Lake Herald,* 1907-03-05; "Sheets Freed on Technicality," *Salt Lake Herald,* 1907-04-13.

140 Hilton also did a murder trial in Salt Lake City with Christensen as cocounsel. The prosecutor was Elmer Leatherwood. The key prosecution witness was Axel Steele. Hilton significantly impeached Steele's testimony that he was an eyewitness to the murder. "Attempts Made To Find Flaws in Story of Deputy," *Salt Lake Herald,* 1912-10-31.

141 *The Bates Alumnus,* June 1921.

142 In their 2005 statistics, the Masonic Grand Lodge of Utah could muster about two thousand Masons. This is the second-lowest total by state and by far the lowest total in percentage of population. Opening the Lodge to Mormons does not seem to have greatly enlarged their numbers. I have known Mormons and I have known Masons, but I have yet to meet a Mormon of any activity who was a member of the Masons. My Masonic colleague and my clients freely discussed lodge activities but never at any time suggested that an active Mormon might find a home in Masonry.

143 The Community of Christ (formerly the Reorganized Church of Jesus Christ of Latter-day Saints) rejects most of the Nauvoo innovations.

144 Mormons do not talk about the Temple Ceremony, which carries a requirement of nondisclosure. The Latter-day Saint Creation "myth" is set out in clarity in Joseph Smith's *Book of Moses* found in the openly available church published Pearl of Great Price.

145 Kinney, Jay, *The Masonic Myth,* Harper Collins, New York, 2009. See Chapter Seven.

146 The best treatment of Utah Masonry is Michael W. Hunter, "Masonry and Mormonism" *Journal of Mormon History* 18(2) 57–96 (1992).

147 *Bergera v. United States,* 297 F. 102 (8th Cir. 1924).

148 Thompson was represented on appeal by Chief Justice Straup, who had been defeated for reelection. Straup would return to the Court and serve many more years.

Chapter 10

149 "Sensational Charge Made By Judge Hilton, Counsel for Vincent St. John," *Salt Lake Herald,* 1907-05-24.

150 "Allege Court is Prejudiced," *Salt Lake Herald,* 1907-05-26.

151 "Attack Made on Trial Court," *Salt Lake City Herald,* 1915-05-29.

152 *State v. Hill,* 44 Utah 79, 138 P 1149 (Utah 1914).

153 *State v. Brown,* 948 P.2d 337 (Utah 1997).

154 It is hard to second guess after all these years. The federal law on commenting on the failure to take the stand was against Joe Hill and Judge Hilton. They could have and perhaps should have argued the question under the Utah state constitution. Later in the 1930s Justice Straup would find independent state constitutional grounds for extended criminal protection.

155 Flynn, Elizabeth Gurley, *The Rebel Girl,* pp. 192–93.

156 The application is found in the *Utah Digital Archives.* It is a printed form, but it appears that it was filled out in Joe Hill's handwriting.

157 *Mitchell v. United States,* 526 US 314 (1999). "It is true, as a general rule, that where there can be no further incrimination, there is no basis for the assertion of the privilege. We conclude that principle applies to cases in which the sentence has been fixed and the judgment of conviction has become final. If no adverse consequences can be visited upon the convicted person by reason of further testimony, there is no further incrimination to be feared." *See also State v. Anderson,* 495 P.2d 804 (Utah 1972).

158 "Will Hillstrom Give Name of the 'Woman'?" *Salt Lake City Herald,* 1915-09-17.

159 "O.N. Hilton To Argue Hillstrom Case Today," Salt
Lake City Herald, 1915-09-18.

160 "The Case of Hillstrom," *Salt Lake City Herald,*
1915-09-24.

161 "Board of Pardons Condemned by Hilton," *Salt Lake
Telegram,* 1915-09-20.

162 "Hillstrom Refuses to Give Swedish Ambassador Any
New Evidence," *Salt Lake Telegram,* 1915-09-29.

163 Spry was also getting many letters from Utah and
around the world. One of his correspondents was
former President Theodore Roosevelt. "Spry Says Utah
Bar Should Act in Hilton Case," *Salt Lake Telegram,*
1915-12-01.

164 "Rewards are offered," Salt *Lake Telegram,*
1915-09-30.

165 "Challenge to Pardon Board Tacked up throughout
County," *Salt Lake Telegram,* 1915-10-29.

166 The massacre of non-Mormon emigrants near Cedar
City, Utah, in 1856. Mormon settlers were implicated
and Mormon leader John D. Lee executed for the
crime.

167 "Officials Refute Statements by Hilton," *Salt Lake
Telegram,* 1915-10-20.

168 "General News," *Park City Record,* 1915-12-10.

Chapter 11

169 "May Disbar Hilton From Utah Courts," *Salt Lake
Telegram,* 1915-11-28.

170 "Spry Says Utah Bar Should Act in Hilton Case," *Salt
Lake Telegram,* 1915-12-01.

171 "Hilton Disbarment is to be Started in Few-Days," *Salt
Lake Telegram, 1915-12-03.*

172 Nebecker made such a career out of prosecuting this
disbarment case that in the second half of the Wilson
administration, he was appointed Assistant US Attorney.
He, in fact, was the one who prosecuted (or persecuted) the
IWW leadership in Chicago in Judge Kennesaw Mountain

Landis's court. This was the case that led to the imprisonment of much of the IWW leadership and Bill Haywood's skipping bail to go to the Soviet Union.

173 "Charges are filed against Judge Hilton," *Salt Lake Tribune,* 1915-12-21.

174 "Hilton Files Warm Answers; Fights Disbarment," *Salt Lake Tribune,* 1916-02-19.

175 "Hilton Will Stand Upon What He Said," *Salt Lake Telegram,* 1916-02-19.

176 "Argument in Hilton Case Is Heard By High Court," *Salt Lake Telegram,* 1916-03-26.

177 A modern lawyer would look to the provisions of Rules of Professional Conduct, Rule 8.2, which explicitly prohibits a lawyer from casting doubt on the intellect or integrity of a court.

178 *Kentucky v. Berry,* 2011 WL 1376280 (E.D. Kentucky April 12, 2011).

Bibliography

CASES

Adair v. United States, 298 US 161 (1908).

Adamson v. California, 332 US 46

Bergera v. United States, 297 F. 102 (8th Cir. 1924).

Butte v. Illinois, 333 US 640 (1948).

Chandler v. Fretag, 348 US 640 (1948).

Clinton et al v. Englebrecht, 80 US 434 (1871).

Cooke v. Cooke, 248 P. 83 (Utah 1926).

Coppage v. Kansas, 236 US 1 (1915).

Gardner v. State, 234 P.3d 1115 (Utah 2010).

Gideon v. Wainwright, 372 US 335 (1963).

Grant v. Lawrence, 37 Utah 450, 108 P.931 (Utah 1910).

Holden v. Hardy, 169 US 366 (1898).

In re Davis, 246 B.R. 646 (Bk. Utah 2000).

In the Matter of Scott, 296 P. 1113 (Nev. 1931).

In re Hilton, 158 Pacific 691 (Utah 1916).

Kelsey v. District Court of First Judicial District of Platte County, 139 P. 433 (Wyoming, 1914).

Kentucky v. Berry, 2011 WL 1376280 (E.D. Kentucky April 12, 2011).

Lochner v. New York, 198 US 45 (1905).

Malloy v. Hogan, 378 US 1 (1964).

Mapp v. Ohio, 367 US 643 (1961).

Michigan v. Gioglio, 2011 WL 173182 (Mich. App. April 5, 2011).

Minah Consol. Min. Co. v. Briscoe, 89 F. 891 (9th Cir. 1898).

Miranda v. Arizona, 384 US 436 (1966).

Mitchell v. United States, 526 US 314 (1999).

Paul v. Salt Lake City R.R. Co, 34 Utah 1, 95 P. 363 (Utah 1908).

Pettibone v. Nichols, 203 US 192 (1906).

Powell v. Alabama, 287 US 45 (1932).

State v. Brown, 948 P.2d 337 (Utah 1997).

State v. Clopten, 2009 UT 84.

State v. Drobel, 815 P.2d 724 (Utah App. 1991).

State v. Hansen, 734 P.2d 421 (Utah 1986).

State v. Hill, 44 Utah, 79, 138 P. 1149 (Utah 1914).

State v. Hillstrom, 150 Pacific 935 (Utah 1915).

State v. Poole, 232 P.3d 519 (Utah 2010).

State v. Spies, 122 Illinois 1 (1887).

Tinkler v. Powell, 151 P. 1097 (Wyoming 1915).

Toneray v. Budge, 95 P. 26 (Idaho March 1908).

Twining v. New Jersey, 211 US 78 (1908).

United States v. Hastings, 461 US 499 (1983).

United States v. Robinson, 485 US 25 (1988).

NEWSPAPERS

Biographical Directory of the United States Congress

Carbon County News (Price, Utah)

Deseret Evening News

Duchesne County (Utah) Newspaper (Vernal, Utah)

Eastern Utah Advocate (Price, Utah)

Eureka (Utah) Reporter

Kemmerer Camera (Wyoming)

Park City (Utah)Record

Salt Lake Herald

Salt Lake Telegram

Salt Lake Tribune

Solidarity (Spokane, Washington)

Utah Bar Journal

Utah Historical Encyclopedia

BOOKS

Arrington, Leonard, *Great Basin Kingdom*, Harvard University Press, Cambridge, Mass, 1955

Ball, David and Kennan, Don, *Reptile*, Balloon Press, New York, 2009.

Borah, William, *Closing Arguments of W.E. Borah in Haywood Trial*, Boise, 1906.

Brodie, Fawn, *No Man Knows My History*, Alfred Knopf, New York,1945.

Brooks, Juanita, *The Mountain Meadows Massacre*, University of Oklahoma Press, Norman, 1950.

Brooks, John Henry, *American Syndicalism, the IWW*, 1911.

Camp, Helen C., *Iron in her Soul: Elizabeth Gurley Flynn and the American Left*, Washington State University Press, 1995.

Cannon, Frank J., *Under the Prophet in Utah*, 1911.

Carlson, Peter, *Roughneck: The Life and Times of Big Bill Haywood*, W. W. Norton, New York, 1983.

Compton, Todd, *In Sacred Loneliness*, Signature Books, Salt Lake City, 2001.

Conlin, Joseph R., *Big Bill Haywood and the Radical Union Movement*, Syracuse University Press, Syracuse, New York, 1969.

Darrow, Clarence, *Crime: Its Cause and Treatment*, Knopf, New York. 1922.

Doctrine and Covenants, Church of Jesus Christ of Latter-day Saints, Salt Lake City.

Esshom, Frank, *Pioneers and Prominent Men of Utah; History of the Bar and Bench of Utah*, 1913.

Flake, Kathleen, *The Politics of American Religious Identity: The Seating of Senator Reed Smoot, Mormon Apostle*, University of North Carolina Press, 2004.

Flynn, Elizabeth Gurley, *The Rebel Girl: My First Life1906-1926*, International Publishers, New York, 1955.

Foner, Phillip, *The Case of Joe Hill*, International Press, New York, 1965.

Friedman, Rick and Patrick Malone, *Rules of the Road,* Second Edition, Trial Guides, Portland, Oregon, 2010.

Grover, David H., *Debaters and Dynamiters,* Caxton Press, Caldwell, Idaho, 2006.

Haywood, William, *Bill Haywood's Book,* International Publisher's, New York, 1929.

Holbrook, Stewart H., *The Rocky Mountain Revolution,* Henry Holt and Company, New York, 1956.

Holmes, Oliver Wendell Jr., *The History of the Common Law,* 1881.

Jensen, Andrew, *Latter-day Saint Biographical Encyclopedia,* Salt Lake City, Utah, 1979 edition.

Jensen, Vernon H., *Heritage of Conflict,* Cornell University Press, Ithaca, New York, 1950.

Kinney, Jay, *The Masonic Myth,* Harper Collins, New York, 2009.

Lucas, J. Anthony, *Big Trouble,* Simon and Schuster, New York, 1997.

Pipes, Daniel, *Conspiracy: How the Paranoid Style Flourishes and Where it Comes From,* Knopf, New York,1922.

Pearl of Great Price, Church of Jesus Christ of Latter-day Saints, Deseret Book, Salt Lake City, 1920.

MacDougall, Ernest D., *Speculation and Gambling,* The Stratford Company, Boston, Massachusetts, 1936.

Martin, MaryJoy, *The Corpse on Boomerang Road,* Western Reflections Publishing Company, Montrose, Col. 2004

May, Dean L., *Utah: A Peoples History,* University of Utah Press, Salt Lake City, 1987.

Philpott, William, *The Lessons of Leadville,* Colorado Historical Society, Denver, 1994.

Preston, William, *Aliens and Dissenters,* Harper and Row, New York, 1963.

Renshaw, Patrick, *The Wobblies,* Doubleday, New York, 1967.

Roberts, B.H., *Recent Discussion of Mormon Affairs,* Salt Lake City, Utah, 1907: *Comprehensive History of the Church,* Deseret Book, Salt Lake City 1965 Edition.

St. John, Vincent, *The IWW: Its History, Structure and Methods*, Red Dawn Press, Cincinnati, Ohio, 1917.

Smith, Gibbs, *Joe Hill*, University of Utah Press, Salt Lake City, 1967.

Smith, Joseph Fielding, *Essentials in Church History*, Deseret Book, Salt Lake City, 1974.

Spence, Gerry, *Win Your Case*, St. Martin Griffin, New York, 2005.

Stavis, Barrie, *The Man Who Never Died*, Haven Press, New York, 1954.

Stegner, Wallace, *The Preacher and the Slave*, Doubleday, New York, 1950.

Whitney, Orson F., *Life of Heber C. Kimball*, Deseret Books, Salt Lake City, 1888.

Wigmore, John Henry, *Treatise on the Anglo-American System of Evidence in Trials at Common Law*, 1904.

ARTICLES

1921 *Bates Alumnus*.

Hilton, Orin, N., "Crime and Criminals," *Sons of Colorado*, April 1906.

Hunter, Michael W., "Masonry and Mormons," Journal *of Mormon History* 18(2) 57–96, (1992).

Peck, Gunther, "Padrones and Protest: 'Old' Radicals and 'New' Immigrants in Bingham, Utah, 1905–1912," *Western Historical Quarterly*, 24 (May 1993).

Powell, Allen Kent, "The Foreign Element and the 1903–1904 Carbon County Coal Miner's Strike," *Utah Historical Quarterly*, 43 (Spring 1975) 125–54.

Index

May, Dean L., 5, 170
McDowell, Robert, 46
McNamara brothers, 24–25, 31
McWarter, Alexander, 116
mechanization, 14–15
media. *See specific media outlets*
Mexican immigrants, 48
Mexico, Joe Hill in, 2
Michigan Court of Appeals, 110
Michigan Supreme Court, 57
Michigan v. Gioglio, 110, 167
Milken, Michael, 36
miners, importation of, 46
mining enterprises, paranoia of, 145
Miranda v. Arizona, xiii, 168
mistrial, failure to declare in Joe Hill
  case, 161n117
Mooney, Tom, 31
Moore, Fred, 32, 33–34
Moose Lodge, 51, 60, 118
Morgan, James F., 8
Mormonism and Masonry (Goodwin), 120
Mormons and Mormonism. *See also*
  Latter-day Saints; the Church
  attacks on, 144
  beliefs of, 51
  and corporations, 37–43
  deferential treatment of, 42
  and Freemasonry, 119–121,
    163n142
  insecurity of, 50, 52
  and Joe Hill jury, 53
  and jury trials, 76–77
  and labor unions, 148, 149
  on marriage, 155n56. *See also* mar-
    riage; polygamy
  and mining industry, 48, 49
  paranoia of, 143
  as part of Joe Hill story, xvi–xvii
  union war on, 135–136
Morrison, Merlin, 10–11
Morrison, Mr., xiv, 3, 127
Morrison, son of Mr., 3
Morrison's gun, 107
Moslems (American), 51

Mountain Meadows Massacre, 133, 134
movies, depicting juries, 74
Moyer, Charles, 113, 114
Mr. Block (Hill), 21
Murphy, Tom, 8
Myton UT, 59

N
National Consumers' League, 19
National Education Association (NEA), 149
nativism, 45
Nauvoo IL, 48, 80, 119, 120
Nauvoo Stake High Council, 80
Nebeker, Frank, **95**, 139, 140
New Deal legislation, 45
New York legislature, 27
New York Times, 54
Newman, Paul, 74
Nihilism, 116
Ninth Circuit, 126, 147
Nixon, George S., 123
non-admissible evidence, xiii
non-Mormons
  on Joe Hill jury, 37, 53, 77
  lawyers, in Joe Hill case, xx, 77, 132, 133
  in Utah, xvi, 70, 78, 120, 121, 143, 144
Northwest Ordinance, 77
notoriety, 35

O
Oaks, Dallin H., 76
Odd Fellows, 118
Ogden Standard, 38
Orchard, Harry, 30, 113, 114, 115
Otis, James, 73
Owen, Thomas Joseph, 46, 49

P
Palmer, Alexander M., 17
Park City Record, 135, 168
Park City UT, 2
Parrent, Mr., 116
Paul, Louisa P., 40–41
Paul v. Salt Lake City R. Co., 40, 168
Peck, Gregory, 74

Peck, Gunther, 47, 171
Peckham, Rufus W., 27
Pettibone, George, 30, 113, 114, 115
Pettibone dope, 114
phrenology, 118
"pie in the sky," origin of, 23, 68
Pioneers and Prominent Men of Utah
(Eshom), xxi, 83, 169
Pipes, Daniel, 146, 170
polygamy, 38, 43, 50–51, 52, 76, 80,
119, 143
Powell, Alan Kent, 47, 171
Pratt, Orson, 81
Pratt, Parley P., 76
"Preacher and the Slave" (Hill), 23,
68–69
The Preacher and the Slave (Stegner), xii,
4, 171
preemptory challenges, 79–80, 82
presentism, 148
Preston, Thomas, 74
Prince Hall Masonic Order, 119
Progressive Party, 44
progressives and progressivism, xx,
17–19, 38, 44
propaganda, 24–26, 32, 33, 78, 82,
124, 130
Protestantism, ministers accusation
against the Church, 50, 51

R
"The Rebel Girl" (Hill), 70–71
The Rebel Girl: My First Life 1906-1926
(Flynn), 20, 169
Red Dawn Press, 14
relevance, concept of, xiv
Relief Society, 81
religion
Joe Hill on, 68–69
role in Joe Hill case, 69–70
*Reptile: The 2009 Manual of the Plaintiff's
Revolution* (Ball and Kennan), xv, 169
Rich County UT, 81
right to counsel, 111
right to defend oneself, 103

Rio Grande Railroad, 46

riots
Centralia WA, 17
Salt Lake UT, 8
Ritchie, Morris, xiv, xv, 10, 52, 63, 78,
79, **93**, 100, 102, 106, 127
Roberts, B. H., 45, 51, 52, **90**, 170
Robinson, Fred A., 46
Roosevelt, Franklin, 28, 45
Roosevelt, Theodore, 17, 18, 44, 143
Rotary, 118
Rowan, Ed, 56
Rule 1.1, 56, 155n64, 166n119
Rule 1.2, 161n116
Rule 3.6, 123
Rule 8.2, 142, 166n177
Rules of Professional Conduct, 56, 123,
161n116, 161n119, 166n177
Rules of Professional Responsibility, 101
Russia, 20

S
sabotage, 16, 19
Sacco and Vanzetti case, 31, 32–33
Saint Paul MN, 2
Salt Lake City Ministerial Alliance, 144
Salt Lake City UT
and Joe Hill case, 52, 68, 71
Joe Hill in jail in, 3
Orin Hilton contact with, 115,
163n140
prejudice against IWW, 8, 9
press, 7
riot, 144
unpopularity of laboring class in, 64
Salt Lake County UT
jury pool in, 37
Mormon population and philosophy
of, 53, 78
sheriff's office, 7
Salt Lake Herald, xxi, 7, 8, 79, 130, 168
Salt Lake press, 7, 8
Salt Lake Stake,(LDS), 47